How the Light Gets In

How the Light Gets In

A Lenten Project

Stories collected by Black Heritage Trail of New Hampshire
for the Episcopal Church of New Hampshire

Portsmouth, New Hampshire
2019

ISBN: 978-1-938394-35-5
Library of Congress Control Number: 2019913442

Published by
Black Heritage Trail of New Hampshire
222 Court Street
Portsmouth NH 03801
blackheritagetrailnh.org

Produced by
Grace Peirce
Great Life Press
Rye, NH 03870
www.greatlifepress.com

Contributing editors: JerriAnne Boggis, Angela Matthews, Gail Avery,
Valerie Cunningham

Photos courtesy of: Portsmouth Athenaeum, John Benford Photography,
JerriAnne Boggis, Valerie Cunningham, Rose Downes, Angela
Matthews, David J. Murray, Grace Peirce, Joanna Raptis, Sara Schoman,
Portsmouth Athenaeum, Atlantic Media, Black Heritage Trail of New
Hampshire, and others.

"The Thomas Paul Family," "Pomp & Candace Spring," "Richard Potter,"
and "Frederick Douglass in New Hampshire" © J. Dennis Robinson.
Used with permission.

Cover art: Courtesy of Daniel Minter, danielminter.net

PREFACE

When the Reconciliation Commission of the Episcopal Church of NH reached out to the Black Heritage Trail of NH in the fall of 2017 with an invitation to partner on a Lenten project, the board paused—but only for a moment—to determine how a religious purpose might fit with our secular interpretation of history. With full consensus, we agreed to collaborate for what is now a second year, resulting in two series of stories, with prayers and "collects" that follow the church's forty days of Lenten observances.

The collaboration also brought to life in 2018 a Good Friday Walk that focused on fourteen sites along the Portsmouth Black Heritage Trail, reading aloud stories of free and enslaved Black people who had lived and toiled at great personal loss for the accumulation of wealth and privilege by the local White ruling class. Each historic vignette was acknowledged by reciting a collect, then followed by prayer. In 2019, BHTNH and the Episcopal Church of NH added a second similar Good Friday Walk along the Milford Black Heritage Trail. Walks in both cities attracted individuals seeking an exploration of contemporary injustice and longing for reconciliation, healing, and reparations.

The fourteen stories highlighted on the Good Friday Walks were selected from two series of forty stories prepared by BHTNH volunteer writers including: Valerie Cunningham, JerriAnne Boggis, Jody Fernald, Rev. Deborah Knowlton, Richard Alperin, Mary Jo Alibrio, Steve Fowle, J. Dennis Robinson, Eric Aldrich, Edith Butler, David Watters, Darryl Glenn Nettles, Reginald Pitts, Jeff Bolster, Arnie Alpert, and myself. We thank our volunteer editor, Cathy Wolff, for her keen eye and grammatically correct mind! And we are grateful to the Rev. Bob Thompson for his leadership as chair of BHTNH board, for serving as one of the story readers on the Good Friday Walk, then singing (as only he can) to close at the African Burial Ground Memorial park.

Our partners from the Episcopal Church of NH were The Reverends Elsa Worth, Deacon Derek Scalia, Theresa Gocha, Hays Junkin, Canon Gail Avery (Canon for Transition and Community Engagement); Sooky Lassen, James McKim, Dana Dakin, Linda Douglas; The Reverends Zackary Harmon, Jamie Hamilton, Betsy Hess, Nancy Vogele (Chair of the Reconciliation Commission), Robert Stiefel, and Robert Stevens, Rector; The Rev. Anne Williamson, Associate Rector; The Rev. Nathan Bourne, Curate; The Right Rev. Robert Hirschfeld; and Bishop of the Episcopal Church of NH, Lynn Eaton, Assistant to the Bishop.

Special thanks go to The Most Reverend Michael Bruce Curry, Presiding Bishop and Primate, The Episcopal Church, for taking time to pen the thoughtful and thought-provoking introduction to this book. Rev. Gail Avery also deserves special recognition for shepherding this project and serving as liaison between BHTNH and the Episcopal Church. Gail's unfailing compassion and commitment to working through every detail was essential to the success of the project.

We are encouraged by the recognition of this often ignored history by the generosity of all named herein for writing stories and helping to organize them for the websites, by suggesting and assisting in crafting the Good Friday Walk, and by promoting this observance among all the Episcopal churches in the state. We extend our appreciation to all members of the Reconciliation Commission of the Episcopal Church of NH for bringing their moral authority to bear on a long-neglected injustice.

Amen!
Angela Matthews
Project Volunteer for BHTNH

Valerie Cunningham
Founding member, BHTNH

INTRODUCTION

Jesus of Nazareth said it this way:

*"If you continue in my word, you are truly my disciples;
and you will know the truth, and the truth will make
you free." —John 8:31-32*

For centuries, the stories of African-Americans and people of
color across our land have been hidden under a cloak of silence. As
a result, we have known only part of the truth, and we have only
been partly free. That is why stories and meditations like the ones
captured along the New Hampshire Black Heritage Trail are so
important. At last in our day, in the North and in the South and in
every part of America, we are lifting the veil.

This work of reclaiming and sharing lost histories may bring joy
and may bring pain, but it is always holy. It is the only way to
make the long journey from a fragmented humanity toward racial
healing that leads to becoming God's Beloved Community.

Maya Angelou in her poem, "On the Pulse Of the Morning," said
it this way:

*So say to the Asian, the Hispanic, the Jew,
The African, the Native American, the Sioux,
The Catholic, the Muslim, the French, the Greek,
The Irish, the Rabbi, the Priest, the Sheik,
The Gay, the Straight, the Preacher,
The privileged, the homeless, the Teacher
History, despite its wrenching pain,
Cannot be unlived, but if faced
With courage, need not be lived again.*

So keep telling the story, keep speaking truth, keep reclaiming
the past until it is redeemed by the creation of a new future. Then

all will one day know, as St. Paul said, "the joyful liberty of the children of God."

God love you. God bless you. And may God hold us all in those almighty hands of love.

The Most Reverend Michael B. Curry
Primate and Presiding Bishop of the Episcopal Church

How
the Light Gets In

Day 1, Ash Wednesday
Portsmouth, NH

Will Clarkson

(c. 1739 – 1809)
Angela Matthews

To be Sold at Public Vendue,
At the House of Mr. James Stoodly, Innholder in
Portsmouth, on Wednesday the seventh Day of July
current, at Six of the Clock Afternoon,
Three Negro Men and a Boy :
The Conditions of Sale will be in Cash, or good
Merchantable Boards. Portsmouth, July 1. 1761.

*W*ILL CLARKSON was born about 1739 in Africa, perhaps in what is now Senegal.

Kidnapped by slave traders when he was about sixteen years old, he was brought to Portsmouth and sold at auction to local White tanner James Clarkson who gave Will his English name. Will was also enslaved in the home of Peirse Long when Colonel Long purchased both the Clarkson house and Will from the estate of James Clarkson, Jr.

Clarkson served in the colonies' fight for freedom during the Revolutionary War, though he remained enslaved after the war. As a leader in the Black Portsmouth community, Will Clarkson was elected annually on "Negro Election Day" to the position of viceroy in the Black Court, and in 1789 he was elected King of Court. Due to ill health, he stepped down the next year. In 1779, Will had been one of twenty African men to sign a petition to the New Hampshire legislature asking for an end to slavery in New Hampshire. Although the petition was tabled without further action, Colonel Long kept his promise and in his final testament in 1789 made Will a free man.

Will and his first wife Abby, who died in April of 1794, had two children, Naby and William. In 1802 Will married Matilda, Jack Odiorne's widow. South Church records show that Will died on April 17, 1809 at age seventy, having sustained himself on odd jobs, whenever and wherever he could, since gaining freedom.

Collect Day 1 ❦ Will Clarkson

Lord of freedom and life, we raise up today Will Clarkson who fought for the freedom of this country even while enslaved: grant that his service to our country and to the state of New Hampshire may inspire us not to rest until all racism is erased and that true community among all is made a reality; through Jesus Christ our Lord. Amen.

Day 2
Portsmouth, NH

Prince Whipple, The Child

SLAVES PACKED BELOW AND ON DECK.

(c. 1750 – 1796)
Valerie Cunningham

*H*IS FATHER was respected by the people of the village because he was the king. The ten-year-old heir-apparent was growing up with the privileges of royalty, but he also learned how to interact comfortably with children whose families of workers, artisans and counselors provided continuity to traditions along the Gold Coast of western Africa during the eighteenth Century. Despite hearing whispered tales of mysterious abductions, this boy could not have imagined how one day in 1760 he would simply disappear from the lush hills of Aburi, becoming one of millions of Black youths taken by desperately poor White men with guns to a slave trading fort at the ocean where the terrified girls and boys would be sold to the highest bidder.

After surviving unspeakable horrors, the traumatized child-prince arrived on the opposite side of the world without family or documentation until this "one negro boy" was purchased and he recorded as taxable property belonging to William Whipple of Portsmouth in the Colony of New Hampshire. From that moment, the boy would be called Prince, perhaps because of his reputation as royalty. Or maybe it was his early childhood training to respect himself and to be respectful of others. Indeed, history shows that Prince was a man of distinction in military service during the Revolutionary War, as chief of protocol for civilian social functions, and in the evolving racial politics of Portsmouth when, at the age of twenty-nine, Prince Whipple, along with nineteen other distinguished African men who had been enslaved since childhood, petitioned the newly declared independent state of New Hampshire to grant not only their personal freedom but to end slavery for all others in the state.

Prince Whipple, The Adult

Angela Matthews

To CELEBRATE being one of the signers of the Declaration of Independence, General William Whipple, upon returning home to Portsmouth, planted a chestnut seed on the front lawn of his waterfront mansion. The historical record does not reveal what his body servant, Prince, was doing that day, but surely it was he who helped prepare the ground for that seedling, then watched it growing into the tree that continues today to live and spread its branches across the streetscape.

Prince, of Abori, West Africa, came to live in the mansion in 1760, purchased when he was ten years old by William Whipple, a ship's captain and merchant. By 1777, Whipple had become a Brigadier General in command of the First New Hampshire Brigade and was sent to drive Burgoyne out of New York. Prince accompanied Whipple on that campaign as well as to Saratoga (1777) and Rhode Island (1787). For his service in these battles and ensuing bivouacs, Prince earned distinction as a Son of the American Revolution. Indeed, Prince proved to be an astute student of the

Revolution and of the Declaration of Independence, becoming a trusted leader in the local Black community.

In 1779 Prince and nineteen other African men, all enslaved and brought to Portsmouth when they were children, co-authored and submitted their own erudite freedom statement in the form of a petition to the New Hampshire government, asking that their lifetime of servitude be ended, "whereby we may regain our liberty and be ranked in the class of free agents and that the name of slave may not more be heard in a land gloriously contending for the sweets of freedom." The state legislature tabled the petition and never acted on emancipation until 2014 when Gov. Maggie Hassan signed a bill posthumously freeing the men.

On February 22, 1781, Prince married a freed-woman, Dinah Chase, in a ceremony performed by Dinah's former owner, the Rev. Chase of Newcastle. Prince Whipple gained his freedom in 1784 and continued living with his wife and children in his own small house, overlooking the Whipple mansion's flower gardens and the little chestnut tree.

Collect Day 2 ☡ Prince Whipple

O God, our true ruler and guide, we remember today Prince Whipple who sacrificed his life for the freedoms we all now enjoy: grant that as he and other Black citizens petitioned bravely for the end of lifetime servitude in New Hampshire, that we may engage our public servants to end all discrimination so that "the name of slave may no more be heard in a land gloriously contending for the sweets of freedom;" who lives and reigns with you and the Holy Spirit, one God, now and forever. Amen.

Day 3
Mason, NH

Boad

JerriAnne Boggis

A COMMONLY ACCEPTED date for the end of slavery in New Hampshire is 1857, when an act was passed stating that "No person, because of decent, should be disqualified from becoming a citizen of the state." The act is interpreted as prohibiting slavery. By a strict interpretation, however, slavery was outlawed only on Dec. 6, 1865, when the 13th amendment went into effect.

The existence of enslaved Africans is often seen in early town histories as footnotes. These minor or tangential comments marking the lives of Black men, women and children contrast sharply with the lengthy accounts of a wide array of White townsfolk in innumerable town histories dating into the 20th century.

In Ramsdell's *History of Milford*, what we know of an enslaved child appears as a footnote to the story of one of the town's early resident. "Captain Josiah Crosby came to Milford in 1753, he brought with him two children one White and the other colored. They named the child Jeffrey and sold him at the age of five when they moved to Billerica."

An earlier documentation for the year 1743 seen in Rothovius' book, *The Lodge*, introduces Boad: "While the Groton residents never actually settled in the Gore, they drove cattle up each spring to pasture in the meadows of Spaulding Brook. A Negro Slave named Boad looked after these cattle and the site of his 225-year-old cabin is probably marked by a rude foundation on the Mason side of the Mile Slip's western line."

In 2008 on the Mason town green a statue of Bode was erected and dedicated to Elizabeth Orton "Twig" Jones (1910-2005), a renowned illustrator and author of children's books and former Mason resident. Her description of Boad in the 1968 *Mason Bicentennial History* adds flesh to the bones of an annotation.

> Every year in late winter, several Groton families would send up their young cattle under the care of Boad (sometimes spelled Bode) a Negro slave. Boad, perhaps only a boy, would drive the cattle through the forest from Groton to Nose Meadow where he would camp for months all alone, hunting, fishing, gathering berries for his food, while the cattle grew fat on the plentiful vegetation of this wilderness. Sometimes he would burn over an area to promote succulent new growth for the cattle. Parties of Groton people would come up in midsummer to cut and stack hay. In the fall they would come again. But most of the time Boad was the sole inhabitant of what is now Mason, all summer long, under the stars at night, under the sun by day, in the midst of storms, thunder and lightning and pouring rain. Sometimes the hideous howls of wolves filled the air. Boad heard owls screeching, foxes barking, wild turkeys gobbling. What were his thoughts? We know very little about him. In the early church records of Groton, long after his duties of bringing the young cattle to Nose Meadow were over, we find under MARRIAGES – February 5, 1750: Bode to By (Negro servants of Groton). Still later, in a list of members of the Church of Christ in Groton, we find, down in the corner of the page, away from the other names: Bode Negro. There were fourteen Negro slaves in Groton, Boad being the only one listed as a church member. From 1734 through 1740, so far as we know, Boad brought up the cattle every year.

The scant notation "Bode to By" was probably considered a sufficient record for the marriage of an enslaved couple. However, what we know from these short writings is that African Americans lived full lives — they worked, they married and they had families. We are thankful for these scant references for without them the lives of these early New Hampshire residents would have been forgotten, erased forever.

Collect Day 3 ❦ Boad

O God, who sent shepherds forth to care for all people: we remember today Boad who while enslaved cared for cattle in the midst of the abundant fields of Mason, New Hampshire; grant that we may become shepherds of truth and honor as we remember all those whose life and work built our communities though we easily forget them at our peril; through Jesus Christ our Lord. Amen.

Day 4
Jaffrey, NH

Amos Fortune

(c. 1700 – 1801)
Angela Matthews

HANNAH DAVIS - AMOS FORTUNE

Buried behind Jaffrey's colonial Meeting House nearby are "Aunt" Hannah Davis, 1784-1863, resourceful and beloved spinster who made, trade-marked and sold this country's first wooden bandboxes; and Amos Fortune, 1710-1801, African-born slave who purchased his freedom, established a tannery and left funds for the Jaffrey church and schools.

Amos Fortune is described as an exemplary citizen of New England. Born in Africa in the early 1700s, Fortune was brought to the colonies to be an enslaved servant and became the property of Ichabod Richardson, a tanner in Woburn of Massachusetts-bay. An unsigned "freedom paper" dated December 20, 1763 promised Amos his freedom at the end of four years of service, but it is not a promise stated in Richardson's will upon his death in 1768 and it was not honored by Richardson's heirs. Amos later negotiated a price for his freedom and made his final payment in 1770 at the age of 60.

Fortune bought land and with the help of his former owner built a house for himself and his first wife Lily Twombly, whose freedom he had purchased from Josiah Bowers. Sadly, Lily died within a year. On November 9, 1779, Fortune purchased the freedom of Violate and they married the next day. Two years later they moved to Jaffrey NH where Fortune established a successful tannery and took on at least two apprentices, serving clients in Massachusetts and New Hampshire. In 1785 Amos and Violate adopted a daughter, Celyndia. In 1789 Fortune purchased 25 acres on the Tyler Brook where he built their house and a tannery barn, both still standing in Jaffrey.

Fortune and the Rev. Laban Ainsworth became good friends and co-founders of the Jaffrey Social Library, whose members met Saturday evenings to collect and discuss books dealing with history and travel. Fortune was a full member of the First Church in Jaffrey. In his will he left a "handsome present" to the church and another to support the town Schoolhouse Number 7. Today, that fund is called the Amos Fortune Fund to support projects including public speaking contests and special publications. The Jaffrey Public Library administers the Fund, using the income to develop and distribute educational materials about Amos Fortune.

Archival documents attest to Fortune's literacy, professional skills, community position, and financial success. The Rev. Laban Ainsworth wrote the epitaphs on Amos' and Violate's headstones when they passed away a year apart. He wrote, "*to the memory of Amos Fortune, who was born free in Africa, a slave in America, he purchased Liberty, professed Christianity, lived reputably, and died hopefully, November 17, 1801, AEt. 91.*" And of Violate Ainsworth wrote, "*to the memory of Violate, by sale the slave of Amos Fortune, by marriage his wife, by her fidelity, his friend and solace, she died his widow, September 13, 1802, AEt. 73.*"

Collect Day 4 ❦ Amos Fortune

O God of true justice and peace: we remember today your free servant Amos Fortune who paid for his freedom from enslavement and then contributed much to the community of Jaffrey in founding a library and supporting public education and the maintenance of the church; may we boldly confess the gifts of all citizens woven into a beautiful fabric from all races that enrich our lives and open our minds to the truth of your goodness; through Jesus Christ our Lord. Amen.

HOW THE LIGHT GETS IN

Day 5
Newington, NH

Corydon Chesley

(c. 1740 – 1831)

Jody Fernald

J O I N, or D I E.

*C*ORYDON CHESLEY was
born into slavery in Newington, around 1740. His first owner was Joseph Adams Jr., the son of the Rev. Joseph Adams, one of New Hampshire's most prominent ministers from the Puritan-inspired school of thought. Adams had Corydon baptized into the church in 1750 as his predecessors had done in their hierarchical embrace of saving all souls even those at the lowest rung of society. Six years later, Adams sold Corydon through the slave trader William Shackford of Newington. Corydon was 16 years old and would have fetched a high price as a laborer with a long future ahead of him. James Chesley, a prosperous farmer of Dover, purchased Corydon. Ironically, John Rowe's book, *Newington, New Hampshire,* is subtitled, "*a heritage of independence since 1630.*" Clearly the heritage belonged to the dominant population.

When James Chesley died in 1777, Corydon was listed as property in the estate inventory at a value much reduced from his original sale value. Corydon was approaching age forty and considered of less importance to Chesley's young widow, Lydia. Early in 1778, Corydon enlisted in the Revolutionary Army in Captain John Drew's company of the 2nd NH Regiment. The promise of freedom enticed many Black men in New Hampshire to enlist. Corydon would have been paid a bounty at enlistment and likely used that money to purchase his freedom from Lydia two weeks later. The Rev. Jeremy Belknap issued the manumission papers, and it is in Belknap's Church in Dover, where Corydon's daughter would later join Dover's Ladies' Antislavery Society. Corydon Chesley served in the military for three years, fighting in Monmouth, Western Pennsylvania and New York. He served with five other Black men: Richard Hunking, Zach Kelsey, Cato, Gloster Watson and George Evans.

Often history has lost track of the Black men who emerged from slavery in New Hampshire. Corydon, however, married Judith Cole of Somersworth, NH, a White woman, and had several children. Corydon applied for pension benefits and received a land bounty. He sold that land and stopped receiving a pension benefit when he could not prove that he suffered poverty. He and his wife attended church in Portsmouth, and he died on March 1, 1831 at ninety-one years old.

Please see Glenn Knoblock's fine book *"Strong and Brave Fellows": New Hampshire's Black Soldiers and Sailors of the American Revolution, 1775-1784*, the source of much of the information in this essay as well as on other Black men in New Hampshire.

Collect Day 5 ☙ Corydon Chesley

Almighty and everlasting God, you choose those whom the world deems powerless to put the powerful to shame: we remember today your free servant Corydon Chesley who fought bravely for the freedom of this country while he himself was enslaved; may we never forget the sacrifices of the African Americans who gave us the gift of freedom so that the shame and sin of racism may end in our communities and nation; through Jesus Christ our Lord. Amen.

Day 6
Portsmouth, NH

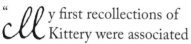 Dinah Gibson

(c. 1742 – 1825)
Valerie Cunningham

"**My** first recollections of Kittery were associated with Dinah. My Grandfather Rice bought her when she was eighteen years old & she remained faithful & devoted to the family until her death in 1825 or 6." Sarah Parker Rice Goodwin wrote this in her memoirs titled *Pleasant Memories*.

Dinah's life is a reminder that the story of Black people in Kittery is one and the same as their story in Portsmouth, dating back as far and involving the many people who moved back and forth across the river. These known stories omit significant details of daily life. And Dinah's first recollections of Kittery surely were not one and the same as Sarah's.

This we know: Dinah, formerly enslaved by the Rice family of Kittery, worked in Portsmouth, making a living from her culinary knowledge. She catered events at the Assembly House ballroom where Whipple slaves also appeared, Prince as the major-domo and Cuffee as violinist. Sarah Goodwin described how Dinah's "sandwiches of tongue and ham, with thin biscuit, were handed round on large waiters, in turn with sangaree, lemonade, and chocolate . . ." and Dinah would explain " . . . how long they boiled the chocolate, which had spice in it."

Advertisements in *The New Hampshire Gazette* inform us that enslaved women working in the mansions of Portsmouth's seaport merchants had access to a world of imported delicacies, enabling them to reinvent African cookery, seasoning foods with subtlety and complexity not indigenous to Anglo-American food ways. People like Dinah were gaining their freedom in post-revolutionary Portsmouth, and some newly emancipated slaves could continue to live in the town if they were able to find work-for-wages within a designated time. The city was regaining prosperity after the war and it remained the leader of fashion in the region with many scenes of banquets, balls, and festive occasions to fill the new function halls on Congress Street.

No description has been found of Dinah's wedding day, other than the North Church minister recording the marriage of John Gibson to Dinah on August 20, 1804. Both John and Dinah eluded the compilers of the first city directory in 1821. But this we know about Dinah, that she was living in the area until February 1825, because her funeral was recorded in North Church records: "Dinah Gibson found dead on ice near her home, fell in the night, Froze."

Collect Day 6 ❦ Dinah Gibson

O God, you open your hand and feed us richly from your creation: we remember today your free servant Dinah Gibson whose culinary skills and grace fed many even while she was enslaved; may we in her memory feed each other with the truth of how much our lives and freedoms depended upon those we have overlooked or forgotten so that no one is left behind; this we ask in the name of our Lord Jesus Christ whose table was open to all. Amen.

Day 7
Hampton & Epping, NH

Cato Fisk & Jenny, "A Negro Servant"

Rev. Deborah Knowlton

ONE MIGHT wonder how or why Puritan clergymen of the 1700s came to own slaves. It seems counter-intuitive for those who fled England and its repressive belief systems, to exult in a setting that gave them freer self-expression, while at the same moment make a choice to enslave another human being. One reason may have been buried in the scriptures that were so important to Puritans. There, slaves are spoken of as simply another segment of the population and there is no prohibition against owning a slave — only the caution to treat a slave well. Perhaps another impetus for clergy slave-owning was simply the need for labor. Clergy were often paid in land parcels, sometimes as large as 200 acres. They would have needed extra hands to clear stumps, sow oats, flax and hops, and it took years to grow a child who could handle such tasks. Many fervent Christian leaders also argued that to take a "heathen" from a foreign land and place him/her in a Christian home where the gospel was heard, would be good for their soul.

Although their reason is unknown, Ward and Joanna Cotton, owned Jenny. She was baptized at about thirty years old only to die ten years later of the "wind cholick." Jenny is the first "Negro servant" who belonged to a pastor to be listed in the Hampton church records. Since only her baptism and death are noted, it is not possible to do more than conjecture as to what her role was in the family. But the year that Jenny died, 1751, was also the year that Elizabeth Cotton, daughter of Ward, married Ebenezer Fisk and moved to Epping. There they owned Cato Fisk, a Black man, whom they freed about the time of the Revolutionary War. Cato enlisted in 1777 as a drummer but when he got home, picked up his fiddle.

Cato was discharged in 1783 with a Badge of Merit. He married Elsa Husow, a Black woman, in Brentwood with Rev. Nathaniel Trask officiating. They had three children and experienced the same impoverishment that many other Black veterans faced following military service. They moved often as a family and were "warned out" of Poplin, Exeter, Raymond, and Deerfield. So many moves must have left the family with little income and only infrequent, barely adequate shelter. Cato did receive some of his pension, declaring that his whole estate included little more than a small hut, 1 cow, 1 pig, chairs, 2 tables, a scythe, ax and some cooking utensils. At his death in 1824, a service in Epsom was held for both Cato and General Michael McClary who had died about the same time. Offense was taken by some worshippers when the pastor, in his sermon, mentioned Cato's name before that of the general. But, Cato and not the general had been owned and freed by one pastor's child, married and buried by another.

Collect Day 7 ❦ Jenny and Cato

Almighty God, you have given us this good life as our heritage.
However, we do not always act as people mindful of your favor
and glad to do your will. We think of Jenny, who spent her years
living a life that was fashioned by the whims and needs of others.
She was brought to New England as a child, from a place with
a different tongue. Her name was changed and her life marked
only by the cause of her death. Her owners chose not once but twice
to own another human being. We fail you, God, when we choose
disrespect and privilege over equality and respect. We beg your
pardon for the blindness of our ways, especially those of us who
already call ourselves, "devout." Amen

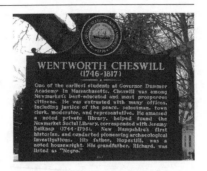

Wentworth Cheswell

(1746 – 1817)

Richard Alperin

ENTWORTH CHESWELL — teacher, coroner, scrivener, assessor, auditor, moderator, selectman and Justice of the Peace — was the only child born to Hopestill and Catherine (Keniston) Cheswell, in Newmarket.

Wentworth's grandfather, Richard Cheswell, enslaved in Exeter, purchased 20 acres of land from the Hilton Grant. The deed, dated Oct. 18, 1716, is the earliest known deed in New Hampshire which shows land ownership by a Black man. The land was located in what was to become the town of Newmarket. Richards only child, Hopestill, was a housewright who plied his trade mostly in Portsmouth. Research has shown he took part in building the John Paul Jones House. Hopestill was active in local affairs and passed his love and knowledge of carpentry, agriculture, and community involvement to his son.

Wentworth attended Dummer Academy in Byfield, Massachusetts. His education was, in terms of the day, "an unusual privilege for a country boy of that time." After completing his education, Wentworth returned home to become a schoolmaster.

In 1765 he purchased his first parcel of land from his father. By early 1767, he was an established landowner, educated, and held a pew in the meetinghouse. He married 17-year-old Mary Davis of Durham, New Hampshire on September 13, 1767. Eleven months later, Paul, the first of 13 children, was born.

During the war for independence, the citizens of Newmarket,

including Wentworth, were unequivocally for the patriotic cause. In April of 1776, along with 162 other men, Wentworth signed the "Association Test," which was uncommon for a man of mixed descent. He was elected town messenger for the Committee of Safety, which entrusted him to carry news to and from the Provincial Committee at Exeter, the state capital at the time.

Paul Revere rode into Portsmouth to alert the colonists of the impending arrival of the British frigate *Scarborough* and the *Canseau* sloop of war. Portsmouth cried out for help from neighboring communities, prompting Newmarket to hold a town meeting. At that meeting it was decided that thirty men be sent to Portsmouth for assistance. Wentworth then rode to Exeter to receive instructions from the Provincial Committee on where the men were to be sent.

Wentworth enlisted in the cause on Sept. 29, 1777. He served under Colonel John Langdon in a select company of "men of rank and position," called "Langdon's Independent Company of Volunteers," to bolster the Continental Army at the battle of Saratoga.

After his service, Wentworth returned to Newmarket and continued his work in local affairs. He also owned a store (which still stands today) beside the old school house. Wentworth's career as a teacher was short lived, but his concern for the educational welfare of Newmarket's children was paramount. In 1776 the town chose Wentworth and four others for a school board to regulate its schools.

He was a man of many firsts. It has been suggested that he was the first archaeologist in New Hampshire. In 1801 Wentworth and several other men in town organized the first library in Newmarket. Wentworth's interest in his town and its history prompted him to hand copy all of the extant town records, including two congregational meetings held in Newmarket. He collected stories and took notes of town events as they occurred. This original work is still intact and is archived at The University of New Hampshire.

Cheswell was appointed as Justice of the Peace for Rockingham County, serving from 1805 until his death in 1817. He was responsible for executing deeds, wills, and legal documents and was a justice in the trial of causes.

In 1820, New Hampshire Senator David Lawrence Morril addressed Congress, being opposed to an item before the legislation concerning persons of mixed race being forbidden to enter or become citizens of Missouri. In his speech Morril remarked that "In New Hampshire there was a yellow man *[sic]* by the name of Cheswell who, with his family, were respectable in points of abilities, property, and character. He held some of the first offices in the town in which he resided, was appointed Justice of the Peace for that county, and was perfectly competent to perform with ability all the duties of his various offices in the most prompt, accurate, and acceptable manner." Angrily, Morril added, "But this family is forbidden to enter and live in Missouri."

Upon writing his will, Cheswell stated that "the burying place in the orchard near my dwelling house be fenced with rocks, as I have laid out (if I should not live to finish it) and gravestones be provided for the graves therein . . . ." His daughter Martha, being his last surviving heir, willed that "the burying yard at my farm as now fenced in, for a burying place for all my connections and their descendants forever . . . on the express condition that they and their heirs and assigns shall forever maintain and support the fence around said burying yard in as good condition as it now is." In accordance with their wishes, the gravestones have been restored or replicated over the last several years, as friends and family have recently discovered their heritage and connection to the Cheswells.

On March 8, 1817, Wentworth Cheswell died from typhus fever. The Newmarket community mourned this vital, important and influential man. Wentworth's own abilities certainly inspired his successful life. However, his father's legacy to his son must not be overlooked. Hopestill's example of hard work, sound investing and determination ultimately helped Wentworth become the successful man we honor.

Collect Day 8 ❧ Wentworth Cheswell

Almighty God, who raised up your servant Wentworth Cheswell to serve the cause of American freedom and to serve his community with honor and dedicated labors in education, government and the pursuit of justice: we pray that his enduring spirit may fill our hearts for service in the cause of true freedom for all the citizens of New Hampshire and of the United States; through Jesus Christ our Lord. Amen.

Day 9
Kensington & Exeter, NH

Jude Hall

(1747 – 1827)
Rev. Deborah Knowlton

HEN JUDE HALL escaped from his owner, Nathaniel Healy, he joined the army and became one of the longest-serving soldiers of the Revolutionary War. He earned his freedom and $100 for his military service from 1775 until 1783. His birth date is uncertain, possibly between 1744 and 1755. He had been enslaved by two men — Philemon Blake, Jr. of Kensington and Healey of Exeter.

Following his years in the military, Jude turned his attention to family and neighbors. The years immediately following the Revolution were difficult for all veterans, but especially so for African Americans. The post-war currency was land. If you did not own a parcel of land, you had precious little of the resources needed to grow food or to build a shelter for yourself and to sustain a family. Few towns had the means to support the poor and the practice of "warning out" was common. If you were warned out, you were required to pick up your belongings and move beyond the town boundaries. Jude, who had just married Rhoda Paul in 1786, was warned out of Exeter in this fashion in 1787. He returned, and together they raised ten children in a cabin in the woods on present-day Drinkwater Road in Exeter — but not before having been warned out of both Stratham and Exeter, again.

Jude and Rhoda had few material possessions — some small pieces of furniture, tongs and earthenware dishes. To maintain his family, Jude fished in a small pond that still exists today, located near his cabin. He also cut lumber and offered manual labor to surrounding farmers. The farmer across the street from Jude owned several acres of woodland which needed cutting. His probated will asks that the executor pay in-full from his estate for his work. Another neighbor, Jonathan Melcher, was taken to court by Jude for breaking into his cabin, ruining the front door and using abusive and threatening language with his wife and children. In 1822 two other neighbors, John Blaisdell and John Wadleigh were alleged to have had an altercation over a sleigh that resulted in Wadleigh's death. Jude carried the injured Wadleigh into his cabin to warm him while Blaisdell went home to tend his cattle. Wadleigh died while in Jude's care. The government won its case against Blaisdell, dependent in great part upon Jude's turns in the witness box — the testimony of a former slave notable for having been judged more truthful than that of a White man.

Although Jude Hall was described as a man of great physical strength, earning himself the nickname, "Old Rock," by 1828 war injuries had caught up with him; he died and was buried in the northeast corner of the Old Yard in Exeter. Later, bounty hunters kidnapped and sold three of Jude's children into slavery, even though they were free people. Jude's son, George, remained in Exeter and marched through the streets in 1857 during the celebration of the abolition of slavery in New Hampshire. Two of George's sons, Moses and Aaron, fought for the Union in the Civil War, continuing the tradition of honor and patriotism in the Hall family.

Collect Day 9 🕯 Jude Hall

You invite us, Lord, in this holy season of Lent, to the practices of prayer, fasting, and self-denial; to the reading of and mediating upon Your holy Word. Jude Hall, his wife and ten children, fasted often, but it was not a fast of choice. They may have mediated upon Your holy Word, and asked You to protect their kidnapped children, to take away the arrogance of a mind that could believe a youth was there for the stealing. Infect us with compassion for the whole human family; take down the seas that separate us; unite us in bonds of love. Help us not to lose strength for the struggle that is always before us—that of making all nations and races one in our desire to serve you; free to sit, cooling our toes together, in the same small ponds. Amen.

Day 10
Canterbury, NH

Sampson Moore Battis

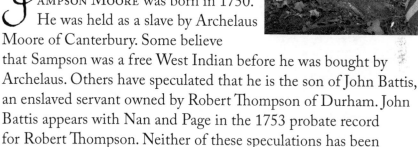

(1750 – 1853)
Rev. Deborah Knowlton

SAMPSON MOORE was born in 1750. He was held as a slave by Archelaus Moore of Canterbury. Some believe that Sampson was a free West Indian before he was bought by Archelaus. Others have speculated that he is the son of John Battis, an enslaved servant owned by Robert Thompson of Durham. John Battis appears with Nan and Page in the 1753 probate record for Robert Thompson. Neither of these speculations has been confirmed.

Sampson was said to have been over six feet tall and a good fiddler. So in 1775, when Canterbury needed its quota of soldiers, he enlisted, served several short terms and was discharged in 1781. There may have been some confusion, since he was listed as a deserter but said he was "verbally" discharged two days before the rest of the unit. Prior to enlistment, his owner, Archelaus, had promised him his freedom for "good fighting." That promise was kept, and Sampson was also given a 100-acre lot in the southwest corner of Canterbury. He was given the honorific title of "Major" by Governor Gilman and was known to have greatly enjoyed the election muster days he attended regularly. His son-in-law, Toney Clark, also a fiddler, was said to have acted as inspector general on traditional muster day celebrations, as well as "dancing master." One wonders if Toney, who lived west of Concord, and Sampson, who lived north of Concord, would meet to enjoy the Concord musters together.

Sampson married Lucy Carey, a West Indian woman owned by William Coffin of Concord. Sampson worked for William for one year in order to purchase Lucy's freedom. It was said by Concord people that Sampson was "well recollected." They had at least three children, possibly as many as seven: Lucinda who married Toney Clark; Sophia who married William Robinson; Peter who married Lydia Harvey; Eliza who married Ephraim Haskell; Sampson, Jr. who married a White woman from Lebanon; and Naomi, and Silas. The Battis family homeplace became known as New Guinea because of the several generations of their children who were born there.

As happened with many other Black veterans, Sampson did not ask for his pension until years after his service. When he did ask in 1832, he was eighty-two years of age; he was placed on the pension rolls in February of 1833. It is said that Sampson lived until 1853 making him 103 years old at his death. If this is true, he far outlived the length of time that he received a pension. Sampson may not have had a birth certificate, or even a death certificate, but his legacy is in the resiliency of the many branches of his family who survived him. Sampson is buried in the southwest corner of the Moore burial ground at Canterbury Center, his grave marked by a White marble headstone, thanks to the vision and dedication of Canterbury's citizens toward marking every gravesite in town of a known patriot.

From Chandler Potter's *Military History of Hew Hampshire*, we learn that Battis achieved the rank of Major when he was given command of a battalion by Governor Gilman in 1800. This probably makes him the first African American to be put in charge of a White troop and to be officially awarded this particular military title; a fact historians have not yet flagged.

Collect Day 10 ❦ Sampson Moore Battis

O God who never forgets the saints who lived in times past: we remember today Sampson Moore Battis who fought for the freedoms we now inherit and who labored for freedom of the woman he loved; may we, like him, raise up generations of youth who speak and act boldly for the honor of all people and who will not tolerate racism in any form; through him who is the way, the truth and the life, our Lord Jesus Christ. Amen

Day 11
Portsmouth, NH

The Portsmouth African Burying Ground

(c. 1700)
Mary Jo Alibrio

*W*HEN VISITING the African Burying Ground in Portsmouth, the misery of slavery (yes, even in New Hampshire) weighs heavily. Feelings of shame, anger and deep sorrow can arise. But stay a little longer in this place; sit quietly on one of the curved concrete benches; look and listen deeply as the possibility of hope and healing unfold.

In this Northern-most shipping port during the seventeenth and eighteenth centuries, enslaved people were sold at auctions in local taverns, along with furniture, tools, and dry goods. After death, they were buried either on the property of their owners or in a segregated plot of land close to the poor house, which was on the outskirts of town.

We know this because of the life-long research of citizen-historian Valerie Cunningham and members of the Portsmouth Black Heritage Trail. In 1995 they included the burying ground as a site on the Trail map and on guided tours. By 2000 the Trail had installed a bronze marker on the corner of Chestnut and State Streets, now a neighborhood of homes and businesses. Research indicated that this was the site of the segregated burial ground for Black residents of Portsmouth.

In Colonial Portsmouth, segregation applied in death as in life. The town government in 1705 documented the location of a separate "Negro Burying Ground" at what was then the outskirts of town. Later descriptions indicate that the cemetery occupies an area between State and Court Streets, west from Chestnut toward Rogers and what was Haymarket Square, or present-day Middle Street. By 1760 Portsmouth's core was expanding into the area of this cemetery. By 1813 the unmarked graveyard was being built over.

One October morning in 2003, during the first hour of work replacing sewer lines on Chestnut Street, the backhoe digging up the pavement struck what appeared to be an unusual piece of wood. The on-call archaeologist soon determined that it was part of a coffin containing human remains. Suddenly, a public works project had become an archaeological site, which eventually revealed multiple burials. DNA testing confirmed that the unearthed bones were indeed of African ancestry. Archaeologists recovered remains of eighteen individuals during the course of the excavation and determined that the site could hold possibly 200 additional burials.

Over the next twelve years, members of the Black "descendant community," city government officials, scientists, artists, local middle school students, church communities, people from the homes and businesses abutting the burying ground, a sculptor, landscape designers, a casket maker, scholars, local funeral homes, and members of civic, business and nonprofit organizations worked together to create an appropriate and permanent memorial designed to re-inter the remains and to honor all the people buried in that place. While it wasn't always a smooth, easy or fast endeavor, a spirit of cooperation and mission among the various constituencies, the racial and cultural backgrounds of the Portsmouth community, kept the project moving and viable.

In May of 2015, completion of the Portsmouth African Burying Ground Memorial on Chestnut Street was marked by holding a public overnight vigil at New Hope Baptist Church, then the consecration ceremony was led by a horse-drawn cortège escorting the caskets to their resting place in the park.

The memorial itself, designed and created by noted sculptor Jerome Meadows, extends an entire city block. At the entry, a life-size sculpture depicts two adults standing back to back. The female figure represents Mother Africa remembering her children to the West, while the male figure facing East stands for all people of the African Diaspora—they are reaching back for each other. What at first appears to be a simple red stone path is actually inscribed with words from a petition for freedom written in 1779 by twenty African men enslaved in Portsmouth.

That path leads to the burial vault marked with a Sankofa, a West African symbol which means "Return and get it. Learn from the past." In the vault, bones and pine coffin remains that had been disturbed earlier were re-interred in hand-crafted caskets. At the far end of the memorial is a railing full of tiles depicting African symbols. With the guidance of Jerome Meadows, the tiles were designed and drawn by middle school art students in Portsmouth. Standing in a semi-circle behind the burial vault are eight shapes, designated as community figures, representing all people who honor and remember those buried beneath this ground. Each figure carries a different message that, together, acknowledge a painful past and hope for a more just future.

They say:
I stand for the Ancestors Here and Beyond
I stand for those who feel anger
I stand for those who were treated unjustly
I stand for those who were taken from their loved ones
I stand for those who suffered the middle passage
I stand for those who survived upon these shores
I stand for those who pay homage to this ground
I stand for those who find dignity in these bones

Collect Day 11 🦶 The Portsmouth African Burying Ground

Loving God, Author of our pasts, we thank you for the journeys of our ancestors, especially those who worked without recognition, without freedom, and with little hope. Whatever our condition today, we stand on their shoulders. Help us to remember this profound, simple truth. With gratitude, we affirm the dignity and worth of every child of yours. We name: their work, worthy; their lives, significant; their journeys, an essential link in our lives today. Holy Spirit that ties and binds us, we celebrate today those who were brought here against their will and were buried in the Portsmouth African Burying Ground: give us a reverence for their lives, their dreams, the contributions they made to making New Hampshire what it is today. In your name, the Finisher of our faith, we pray. Amen

Day 12
Kingston & Hopkinton, NH

Seco

(c. 1747)
Rev. Deborah Knowlton

*I*T IS NOT often that an historical record remains of the sale and purchase of a human being, especially when the details of that record were dictated by a woman. This is the case with Seco Barnard (Sego) who appears first as owned by John Currier of Kingston in the late 1750s. It is uncertain how long John Currier may have owned Seco, but in his 1757 will, John bequeathed Seco to his wife, Ruth, along with half of his house, the barn and his extensive property and assorted farm animals.

Twenty years later, Ruth sells Seco for the sum of £27 to Joseph Barnard of Hopkinton. She delivers Seco, "aged about thirty years . . . to Joseph and his heirs and assigns forever" by way of a hand-written deed upon which she made her mark in the presence of witnesses, Elijah Clough and Phebe Currier, her daughter-in-law.

Joseph Barnard, was a native of Amesbury, Massachusetts, who moved to Hopkinton in 1766. Since Joseph's father and John Currier's father were both influential men in the history of Amesbury, the sale of Seco could have been understood as an "exchange of goods" between friends — but only by those doing the exchange. Joseph was an industrious man who was said to have worked tirelessly to improve his homestead and Seco was also said to have been quite knowledgeable in husbandry. It is likely Seco would have done a great deal of manual labor on such an estate. But it appears that with the sale of Seco to Joseph occurring at the time of the Revolutionary War, Seco first enlisted and served as a private. Sometime after his military duty, in 1790, Joseph Barnard freed Seco. Hopkinton history records that Seco moved south, into Massachusetts, where he met and married a woman named Phillis.

Seco and his wife apparently moved back to Poplin (today known as Fremont) but like so many other freed slaves, they slipped into poverty and were warned out of Poplin. The town sheriff would have given them notice when they had stayed the allowed numbers of days as set by the town, and they would have been obliged to move to a new setting. So, Seco, Phillis and Phillip, perhaps a son, appear next on the pauper rolls of Kingston. There is included in Hopkinton's history the story of Seco meeting up with Joseph Barnard in Amesbury after Seco had been freed. Seco earnestly desired that Joseph take him back with him (likely as an employee, now that Seco was freed). But, Joseph Barnard "resisted, not feeling at liberty to comply."

There is no record of Seco's death, nor of any pension received for his military duty. What does remain is the record of his being bought and sold at the hands of both men and women, who then did not feel at liberty to employ him but did feel at liberty to rebuff him, warn him out of town and do little to alleviate impoverishment until long after his death, when "county farms" were created to deal with the issue of social welfare.

Collect Day 12 🐝 Seco

God Almighty, you made all the peoples of the earth for your glory, to serve you in freedom and in peace. We believe this to be true. We want peace and the dignity of freedom for each individual, as long as they exist first for us. Seco served you and humankind to make our country free. How could we have missed the fact that he lived as chattel, instead, always more bound than free? Would we make a different decision now? Would we seek peace for Seco that is more in accordance with your gracious will? O, by the ever-living power of your Holy Spirit, may that be so. Amen

Day 13
Hampton, NH

Cesar Long,
Dinah, George,
Alice & Paul

RUN away from his Master, John Moody of Newmarket, a NEGRO Man named Neptune, about twenty eight or nine Years of Age—Had on a Home made Coat, the Forepart lin'd with red Shaloon, a green Jacket, a new Pair of Shoes and blue Yarn Stockings;—has loft two of his Toes, and can't move his Under Jaw. If any Person will take up said Run away, and return him to his Master, or secure him, that he may have him again, he shall be allowed for Charges, and be satisfied for his Trouble, by me the Subscriber, Newmarket, April 21.   JOHN MOODY.

Rev. Deborah Knowlton

*C*AESAR LONG is the first African American listed in the clergy Record Books of the First Congregational Church of Hampton, founded in 1638. Rev. Ward Cotton, seventh pastor of the church made the notation thus, "George Long, son of Cesar a free Negro, was baptized in 1756." This one record, eight words long, can tell us quite a lot about Cesar. We know, for example, that he was a man of faith for whom it was important to have his son baptized. We do not know, however, whether he was seated in the balcony, despite his status as free. The balcony seats were meant for two types of persons — either a person of little status who could not purchase a pew in the front row, or someone considered simple-minded, child-like and therefore, unable to truly grasp the complex theology of the two-hour sermons that were delivered. Cesar's name does not appear in the list of pews, owners and purchase prices, but I do not believe him to have been simple-minded at all.

One wonders if Cesar might have escaped an earlier bondage, since there is an advertisement published in the Boston Gazette of May 1733 concerning a "Negro Man," who had run away from his Master, Richard Long of Salisbury. However, it seems unlikely that a slave on the run would choose to run no farther than the town next door. Rather, Cesar's freedom likely encouraged him to risk putting forth three cases for litigation. In 1757, he was a plaintiff in action against Hollis. In Hampton, he was a plaintiff twice — both cases in which he demanded payment for caring for, first, the Redman family during the smallpox epidemic, and later for Nathan Blake.

We also know that Cesar had children other than George, including Alice and Paul and two infants who died. They must have had a mother, but none is listed in Hampton. However, the North Hampton church records state, "Dinah, wife of Cesar Long" died in 1774 at age fifty-five. Dinah seems also to have been free, simply not living with George and the children. This is advantageous since the children's status as free could only be secured if their mother was free. The cause of Dinah's death is listed as intoxication.

After her death, in 1776, Cesar enlisted in Capt. Samuel Nay's company in Col. Joshua Wingate's regiment, along with his son, Paul. It is believed that George also enlisted — perhaps later. A record from North Hampton indicates that Alice marries William Scott (a man of color) in 1791, has several children and succumbs to consumption in 1810. Paul marries Phebe Swain, has three or more children, all of whom were active in the life of the congregation, but several of whom also died of consumption. Paul must have been well-known in the town of North Hampton for after his wife's death, he became completely blind and the town supported him at lodgings he shared with his sister's husband, William Scott. Cesar Long and his family were faithful, patriotic persons who contributed much to the life of both the Hampton and North Hampton communities.

Collect Day 13 ☙ Cesar Long, Dinah, George, Alice & Paul

You grant us this Lenten season, Lord, as a way to provide us with time to contemplate the most notorious of our sins; especially those that separate us from the rest of the body of Christ. Caesar and his wife, Dinah, lived separated from one another during their married lives, as was the custom of enslaved Blacks even though they were free. Did they wish for reconciliation and forgiveness, for restoration to the sanctity that comes when persons belong wholly to one another? Turn our thoughts to the message of your pardon and absolution set forth in the Gospel in such a way that we let the question, "What kept them apart?" be the same question we ask ourselves . . . "What keeps us apart from wholly belonging to one another in the human family?" Amen

Day 14
Portsmouth, NH

Primus Fowle

(1700 – 1787)
Steve Fowle

NH's first printing press / Courtesy NHGazette.com

CCORDING TO the laws and customs of his place and time, Primus was, in a very literal sense, a man of no account. As a Black African in eighteenth-century New England, he was considered to be mere property in the eyes of the law. Thousands of others who suffered that intolerable condition lived and died in utter obscurity, but not Primus.

For thirty years or more, he was made to pull the lever of a wooden common press, forcing blank paper to accept black-inked type, in the process printers call making an impression. That work made an impression on him — it bent his back so, that he could not stand upright. But, though he was dealt a life of drudgery, and though he died centuries ago, still, something of Primus lives on today. The world did its best to crush him, but he left his impression on the world.

Primus first appears in 1730, his purchase noted in the account book of Hugh Hall. Before, and for two decades after, his life is a mystery. When Hall's daughter Lydia married the printer Daniel Fowle, Primus was, apparently, Lydia's dowry. A few years after the marriage, Daniel and the Massachusetts legislature fell into acrimonious disagreement over "The Monster of Monsters," a scurrilous satirical pamphlet. Under interrogation, Daniel admitted that Primus — "my Negro" — may have been involved in the printing of "the Monster."

HOW THE LIGHT GETS IN

We know this story because Daniel published a pamphlet about being locked up in Boston's "stone gaol." Its tone was indignant rather than jocular, but there's irony in its title: a slave-owning man complaining about "A Total Eclipse of Liberty." Daniel, Lydia and Primus soon moved to Portsmouth, where Daniel established the province's first print shop. Lydia died at age thirty-six in 1761. It was at her funeral that we begin to see Primus as more than a cipher.

According to Portsmouth printer Charles Brewster's *Rambles About Portsmouth*, Primus "mourned the loss of his mistress, and called her "an old fool" for dying. Tobias Ham Miller, yet another printer, gives a fuller account: Primus "inadvertently got on the right hand [of the funeral procession], which in this case, was evidently the wrong side." Through nods and gestures, Daniel tried to get Primus to exchange places.

> "At least," [Daniel] whispered, "'Go to the other side," expecting to be promptly obeyed in so slight and reasonable a request; but, to his surprise and that of the bystanders, Primus screamed out, "Go tudder side ye'se'f, ye mean jade." The master of course complied, and the procession moved off.

Primus didn't even own his own body, but he knew who he was—and so did those around him. On his death in 1791, he achieved a unique distinction for an enslaved Black man: he was eulogized in the very paper over whose pages he had once labored.

He may even have left undiscovered surprises, waiting for us yet. In 2015 a Dartmouth librarian, inspecting a broadsheet printed in Daniel's shop, discovered, written in a faded but elegant hand, the words, "Prime *[sic]* Fowle a man of handsome color 1760."

Collect Day 14 ☙ Primus Fowle

God of all mysteries, we thank you for those who through creativity, ingenuity, and determination, made surprising stands for freedom, dignity and justice. Some, like Brother Fowle, showed courage that upended the expected norm. Then and now, these children of Yours create sparks that lead to justice. May we all know greater justice, greater dignity and our full freedom on this earth; we ask this in the name of Jesus, who sets all people free. Amen.

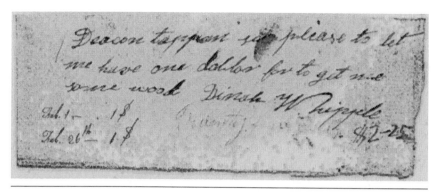

Day 15
Portsmouth, NH

Dinah Chase Whipple

(1760 – 1846)
Angela Matthews

I N 1781 DINAH CHASE WHIPPLE came as a free woman to
marry Prince and to live in the household of William and
Katharine Moffatt Whipple. After Gen. Whipple's death in 1785,
Madam Whipple gave the Black Whipples the use of a small
corner patch of her garden where Prince and, another enslaved
servant, Cuffee Whipple moved their two-story house onto the
lot. There they all lived with their children for the rest of the men's
lives.

Dinah and Cuffee's wife, Rebecca Daverson Whipple, like women
of their station in other African American communities, were
organized to improve life through mutual aid. They founded
the Ladies African Charitable Society, acting in the spirit of a
recollected and passed-down West African tradition of communal
responsibility, where it was understood that helping the individual
helped the community.

They opened a school on the first floor of their house where formerly enslaved adults may have been among the children being taught basic survival skills needed by free people. The school continued into the 1850s by Dinah and her successors in the charitable society. Following the death of her husband in 1796, Dinah continued to support herself until 1832. When living in her house had become a fire hazard, the Whipple family provided Dinah with a small annuity and the use of a house just a few steps away from her church and the neighborhood where she had lived for so long.

Dinah Whipple died in February 1846 at age eighty-six and is buried in Portsmouth's North Cemetery beside her husband, Prince.

Collect Day 15 ❦ Dinah Chase Whipple

Loving God, at Whose command we love and support each other, thank you for those who heard Your call to serve and provided help to those in need, without fanfare and with few resources of their own. These Saints of Yours, such as Dinah Chase Whipple, were Stewards of Your Gifts, claiming and using all they were given to the benefit of Your people. We remember and affirm all of those whose labor provided safety, understanding and dignity for others; in Jesus' loving name, we pray. Amen

Day 16
Newport, NH

Vance Coit

Rev. Deborah Knowlton

NEAR THE END of the 1700s, there was a colony of free Blacks who lived on a hill in Newport. The hill was named after Vance Coit, the leader and most prominent man of the colony. A story passed down about Coit:

> A neighbor, having some hay in a condition in which it would spoil unless taken care of on the Sabbath, applied to Vance for help, offering him a pound of sugar if he would assist in getting it. Vance, with much apparent indignation, replied, "Do you think I would have my soul fry in hell to all eternity for a pound of sugar? No!" He then added, "Give me two pounds, and I will risk it."

Most of the Coit community, or Coit Mountain, residents were freedom fighters who, after escaping enslavement, were simply looking for a place to call home. Among Vance Coit's neighbors were:

Jesse Sherburn, the son of Pomp Sherburne, of Londonderry, who served in the Revolutionary War. Pomp married Florissa Taggart whose freedom he had bought. Their son Jesse was born in 1781. Jesse's parents died early in his life and he was raised by Polly Pinkham until he left Londonderry to join the colony with Vance and the others.

Salem Colby was enslaved to Hannah Bowers of Billerica, who sold him to Lot Colby of Rumford (Concord). After his service in the Revolutionary War, Colby lived at Coit Mountain with his wife and later moved to Vermont.

Tom Billings deserted his wife and moved to Canada with a White woman. An Amma Billings, buried in North Newport Cemetery, may have been Tom's wife.

Charles Hall came from Florida. The story says he secured his freedom by hiding in a sugar barrel on a ship bound for Boston. He was helped by a brother of Deacon Jonathan Cutting. There is a record for a Prudence Hall who died in 1877 and was buried in the same cemetery as Amma Billings. Prudence might have been Charles' wife.

There is no marked area or cemetery where all of these colony members are buried. Only a cellar hole and a rose bush remain as markers to identify Coit's once-thriving mountain colony.

Collect Day 16 Vance Coit

Bringer of all Life, may your holy and life-giving Spirit move the heart of every person to build paths that tie mountain tops to valleys, and to speak words that dismantle the barriers of culture and ethnicity which divide us. Help us to see in the work of Vance Coit, the establishment of a welcoming community for the weary, the war-torn, the unwelcome — any needing refreshment. Invite us to imagine what a beloved community might look like in which suspicions had crumbled away like old stone walls, and hatreds had disappeared, leaving in their place the scent of roses. But may our imagining see, too, not only skin color only—by the varied and beautiful shades of all the skin colors across the globe. Then, spur us to act for such a day, with the help of Jesus Christ our Lord. Amen

Day 17
Exeter, NH

The Thomas Paul Family

(1773 – 1831)
Rev. Deborah Knowlton

Before 1771, Caesar Paul was one of several enslaved men in Exeter freed by his owner, Maj. John Gilman. He married Lovey Rollins of Stratham. Caesar and Lovey had ten children, including Thomas Paul, the eldest of six sons. He and his brothers, Nathaniel and Benjamin, pursued careers in the ministry.

Thomas must have been a dynamic preacher as many churches throughout New England requested him as a guest speaker. In 1804, he received ordination and the next year, he and Catherine Waterhouse were married. They had three children, Ann Catherine, Susan and Thomas, Jr.

Thomas moved his family to Boston where, in 1806, he led the construction and founding of First African Baptist Church, located on Joy Street on Beacon Hill. White people helped with fundraising for the new church, along with many Blacks, including Cato Gardner who donated $1500. Other Blacks did much of the actual construction. Thus, began Paul's ministry career which was to last until his health gave out in 1829. The congregation "loaned Paul out" to assist in the founding of other faith communities such as the Abyssinian Baptist Church in New York. During his tenure Paul also pursued missionary work in Haiti. There, in 1815, under the auspices of the Massachusetts Baptist Society, he laid the groundwork for another church.

Back in Boston, Thomas resumed his ministry and is credited with some of the earliest Black liberation theological work. His adult children continued the family tradition of activism. His daughter, Susan Paul, became a leading member of the Boston Female Anti-Slavery Society and taught local school children, as did her mother. Thomas Jr., was the first Black graduate of Dartmouth College in 1841, then became a teacher and school principal in Boston.

Meanwhile, Thomas' brothers Benjamin and Nathaniel, also Baptist ministers, were involved in abolitionist activities across the region, while another brother Shadrach Paul worked as an itinerant preacher for the New Hampshire Domestic Mission Society in the Epping area.

Thomas Paul died in 1831. Years later, his Joy Street church, known as the African Meetinghouse, was placed on the list of National Historic Landmarks, but not before it served the immigrant Jewish faith community of Anshei Lubavitch, for nearly seventy-five years, until 1972. Thomas Paul would have been delighted!

Collect Day 17 ❦ The Thomas Paul Family

O God, you made us—all the peoples of the earth—of one blood and one breath. You sent your blessed Son to preach peace to those who are far off and to those who are near. Thomas Paul did this for you in Boston, in small towns in NH, in Jamaica, and New York. He went everywhere to encourage others to seek after you and find you. Thomas brought, especially, those of the forgotten nations into your fold. Pour out your Spirit upon us, and bring the day ever closer when we can all live together in your kin-dom, where there is neither slave nor free, male nor female, Jew nor Greek. Bless us when we breathe together as one and our common exhalation is the sound of Shalom. Amen

Day 18
Portsmouth, NH

Pomp & Candace Spring
(1766 – 1807)
J. Dennis Robinson

*A*MONG THE MOST recognized and best loved residents of downtown Portsmouth in its heyday was an African American baker. "Pomp" Spring (he preferred the nickname over "Pompey") was an entrepreneur, civil rights activist, churchgoer and homeowner. Pomp and his wife Candace lived and worked in the heart of Market Square, in a well-kept home a few yards from the North Church.

"He had a town full of friends, black and white," a Portsmouth newspaper eulogized at his death in 1807, "and no enemies that he or anybody else ever knew of."

Born into bondage in nearby Maine, enslaved by the local minister, Pomp Spring stands out — or should stand out — in New Hampshire history as a man of color who lived independently and honorably in a predominantly White world over two centuries ago. Pomp and Candace also remind us that, like most maritime towns, Portsmouth was a more diverse and lively community than the solemn framed portraits of its wealthy upper class imply.

Three times each day, according to nineteenth-century historian Tobias H. Miller, the impeccably-dressed Pomp Spring, driving his perfectly groomed horse, emerged from the narrow Church Street to sell his wares. Pomp was "one of the most genteel, respectable, and highly finished 'gentleman from Africa' ever seen among us in the northern states," Miller wrote in 1852.

In defiance of boilerplate history, Pomp and Candace did not live in an attic or backyard slave quarters. The freed couple owned a comfortable home and operated their once-famous bakery adjacent to the North Church. Pomp's career as a baker was short lived. He died in 1807 at age forty-one. Candace died four months later. The Spring home is gone, but a fascinating room-by-room inventory details every item in their home. What stands out is how typical their worldly possessions were to the White community that surrounded, accepted and admired this fashionable, handsome, hardworking couple.

"He was the baker of bread," Miller wrote. "She was the maker of cakes, for great occasions, grave and gay, among our most genteel people."

At his death the local newspaper eulogized: "Whilst the people of color and especially the poorer class of them, have abundant cause to regret his death, we have no hesitancy to declare that his loss will be felt by all this town."

Collect Day 18 ❦ Pomp & Candace Spring

God of all beauty and creator of all wealth, we are grateful for the entrepreneurial spirit of the Springs, for the example of industry and enterprise that they were to the citizens of our region, and for the memory of excellence they have left for us. They were courageous people, who knew their worth in your eyes. As we reflect on their lives, help us to learn persistence and ingenuity and respect for beauty; in the name of Jesus, we pray. Amen

Day 19
Greenland, NH

Ona Marie Judge Staines

(c. 1773 – 1848)
Angela Matthews

ℬORN INTO ENSLAVEMENT to Betty Judge at Mount Vernon in 1774, Ona Marie Judge became, by five years of age, Martha Washington's favorite personal slave who went everywhere with her mistress.

In November of 1790, a year into the first term of President George Washington, the household, including Ona, moved to Philadelphia, the temporary capital for the government of the newly formed United States.

Pennsylvania's Abolition Act of 1780 required that any enslaved person living in the state for more than six months would automatically become free. The Washington's addressed this law by, prior to the start of the sixth month, regularly exchanging the enslaved at Mount Vernon with the enslaved in Philadelphia. On May 21, 1796, the eve of the household's latest planned exodus from Philadelphia, twenty-two-year-old Ona slipped out of the Executive Mansion while the Washingtons ate their supper and disappeared into the free Black community of Philadelphia. She made her way to Portsmouth, NH, aboard The Nancy, captained by John Bowles, and upon her arrival was met and harbored by the free Black community.

Early in 1797 a local newspaper announcement of recent marriages listed two couples on January 14 . . . "In this town, Mr. John

Staines, to Miss Oney Gudge [*sic*]." Samuel Haven, reverend of Portsmouth's South Church, married them. The Washingtons attempted and failed three times to reclaim their property. The first attempt was thwarted when Washington's nephew explained his plan while dining with Gov. John Langdon. Langdon's trusted servant Siras Bruce aided Ona in her escape to the Greenland home of Phillis and John Jack.

John (Jack) Staines died or disappeared in 1803 leaving Ona impoverished and with three small children. Ona made a meager living as seamstress, washer woman, and house servant. She died in Greenland, New Hampshire, February 25, 1848, at age seventy-four, having outlived her three children, although a son might secretly have left the Seacoast to find a new identity as a free man.

Collect Day 19 ❦ Ona Marie Judge Staines

God of Surprise, we marvel at the courage and ingenuity of Ona Judge. We are grateful for the community of free Blacks and Whites who concealed and supported her. We delight at the truth of such a small woman confounding one who is so mighty. Ona gives us hope. Bless her memory and her deeds. May all who face insurmountable odds find courage and inspiration through her story; in Your Name, who is our Father and our Mother, we pray. Amen.

Day 20
Dover, NH

Dinah, Chloe And Plato Waldron

Jody Fernald

*M*OST HISTORIES of Dover include the Waldron family. From enemies of Native Americans to eminent citizens, the Waldrons have always been included. Those who have not been included in the histories are the family's slaves, including Dinah Waldron and her children, Chloe and Plato, enslaved in the household of Thomas Westbrook Waldron (1721–1785).

The enslaved people of Thomas Westbrook Waldron saw prosperity all around them. Waldron owned extensive landholdings in New Hampshire and Maine, had a close friendship with Gov. John Wentworth and served in many local offices. He owned the Globe Tavern and training grounds at the Portsmouth Plains, as well as numerous pews in the North Church parish in Portsmouth and First Parish in Dover. He rented property to the Rev. Jeremy Belknap, a man whose signature later appeared on the manumission papers of many formerly enslaved people in the area. A portrait by a Boston painter depicts Waldron in sumptuous clothing and surroundings. The painting currently resides in the Historic New England Collections. We have access to Waldron's words and to his image.

There are no existing images of or written words by Dinah and her children. We do not know who fathered the children. We can only imagine their visages and their daily responsibilities. What we do know is that their lives were difficult and held no prospects for improvement. When Waldron wrote his will, he left his "Negro Woman Dinah and her two children Chloe and Plato" to his wife and her heirs forever. Dinah committed suicide by drowning just days after the death of Thomas Westbrook Waldron (Bill of Mortality for Dover from the Society of a Friends). She may have preferred death to the prospect of being passed on as property to the Waldron heirs with the expected separation from her children.

After Dinah's death, prospects remained dim for Plato and Chloe. While Chloe remains an enigma in Dover's history, Plato did leave some traces of his life. He was six years old at the time of his mother's death. In 1797 eighteen-year-old Plato found some silk handkerchiefs and Joseph Gage, a local merchant placed an advertisement seeking the owner. When freed from slavery, Plato Waldron took a job as undertaker and sexton for the First Church in Dover in the early nineteenth century. He married twice, first to Elizabeth Cole of Somersworth in 1810 and second to Elizabeth Kelly in 1834. In 1810 Plato Waldron posted a notice in the Dover newspaper stating that he would no longer be responsible for the debts of his wife. While some feminist historians have found these notices to be published as a means of absolving men of their responsibilities, Plato Waldron's estate inventory revealed numerous debts with local businesses. We don't know the circumstances surrounding his debts. The population of color in Dover in the early nineteenth century was quite small, mostly made up of survivors from enslavement. In 1835 the body of Plato Waldron was found in the Cocheco River. One newspaper reported his death may have been an accident while bathing, or may have been suicide. There were no witnesses.

Thomas Westbrook Waldron was described as "a reluctant patriot" in Revolutionary times. He imagined no life in freedom for his enslaved people. While we discuss the accomplishments of people of color in New Hampshire despite the odds against them, may we

HOW THE LIGHT GETS IN

also take time to memorialize those who did not survive a brutal system and its aftermath.

Collect Day 20 ☙ Dinah, Chloe, and Plato Waldron

God of all Life, we acknowledge the long-unseen lives of Dinah, Chloe and Plato Waldron, seeing in them the lives of too many who were enslaved in New Hampshire and Maine, across the young nation, and even around our world today. They labored, they suffered, they died. We name them when we can, often we still reap the benefits of their labor, in their deaths, help us to give them honor; in the name of God, Who Sees Every Hidden Person and Thing, we pray. Amen.

Day 21
Milford, NH

George Blanchard

(1740 – 1824)

JerriAnne Boggis

G EORGE BLANCHARD, "a colored man," so described in
Ramsdell's *History of Milford*, was a veterinary surgeon and
Revolutionary War vet who moved to Milford from Wilton
in 1804. He was born into slavery in Andover, Massachusetts,
sometime around 1740 and gained his freedom by the time he first
appears in Milford's neighboring town in 1774.

George with his wife, known only as Hannah, were "warned out"
— given official notice by the town fathers that their presence was
not wanted in Wilton. Despite this official discouragement, George
and Hannah decided to stay. Soon after that decision, British
regulars fired on the Minutemen at Lexington & Concord and
George joined the New Hampshire Militia.

Returning from war, Blanchard soon became a tax-paying citizen.
In 1776 he purchased a 40-acre farm and later added an adjacent
30-acre parcel. From the family's modest beginnings, he became
an important animal husbandry resource in the community.
George, who gained enough education to read and to write,
soon became known as an "animal healer," becoming one of the
pioneer veterinarians in the region. "Doctor" Blanchard traveled
through southern New Hampshire and into central Massachusetts
administering treatment to sick animals.

The Blanchards stayed in Wilton until they purchased a 66-
acre plot on the Mason Road in Milford where he became
the town's veterinarian. Curiously, Wright's *History of Milford*,

published seventy-eight years after Ramsdell's, states: "There were no veterinarians recorded in Milford before 1899." In 1805 Blanchard bought the blacksmith shop on Union Square. Wright writes, "This building seems to have come under the ownership of George Blanchard at an early date." Even with the existence of a deed showing Blanchard's ownership of this property, Wright is reluctant to grant credibility to Blanchard as a property owner.

George Blanchard had ten children, all born in Milford. His first wife, Hannah, died in 1779. His widow Elizabeth died in 1832. George had died in 1824 at the age of eighty-four. According to a list of soldiers and sailors published by the Massachusetts Society of the Sons of the American Revolution, Blanchard is buried in Milford in the "Old Burying Ground." His son, Timothy Blanchard, succeeded him as a veterinary surgeon in the town.

On the 1854 map of Milford, Blanchard's farm and the school he donated to the town (District Schoolhouse 4) is identified as the *P.F. Shedd Farm and school*.

In Reginald Pitts' research on the Blanchards, Pitts writes, "By 1830, George's son Timothy was comfortably in the middle ranks of Milford citizens, a family man who owned multiple parcels of land and was involved in a number of business concerns." In less than a decade, however, the family's fortunes would all come to an end. Two days after his forty-eighth birthday, Oct. 3, 1839, Timothy died from an unknown cause and unlike his father did not leave a will. Worse, after his death, his estate went into probate. The administrator started selling off Blanchard's landholdings, pocketing the proceeds. Timothy's family became impoverished, dispersed, and George Blanchard's legacy was erased from Milford's history.

Collect Day 21 ☃ George Blanchard

Almighty God, whose command is to treat one another with loving respect and fairness: witness our sorrow for our failing to acknowledge the success and skill of George Blanchard, and for us failing to protect the inheritance of his descendants. By your Spirit, transform our sorrow into faithful resolve to right the wrongs committed in our names, and to gain wisdom by learning from those we have previously ignored; through Jesus Christ our Lord. Amen.

HOW THE LIGHT GETS IN

Day 22
Portsmouth, NH

The 1779 Petition for Freedom

Mary Jo Alibrio

*M*ANY ENSLAVED PEOPLE in Colonial Portsmouth, New Hampshire, worked in the homes, on the wharves and on the land of influential political figures of the time. Many, including Prince Whipple, also fought in wars along with or in place of their owner.

Prince was bought from slave traders by William Whipple, who would become a signer of the Declaration of Independence. The irony was not lost upon Prince Whipple or the other nineteen enslaved African men who were, themselves, highly regarded Portsmouth community leaders.

Just three years after Thomas Jefferson wrote, "We hold these truths to be self-evident, that all men are created equal, that they are endowed by their Creator with certain unalienable Rights, that among these are Life, Liberty and the pursuit of happiness," twenty Black New Hampshire men, all self-described as born in Africa, composed their own freedom statement as a petition.

The Africans' request to the New Hampshire legislature, meeting at that time in Exeter, was simply to have their humanity recognized and their freedom restored — each having been free when a child. They also stated their prayer for a time "that the name of slave may not more be heard in a land gloriously contending for the sweets of freedom."

The 1779 petition was submitted to the General Assembly in April of the following year. The legislators ordered that it be published in the newspaper "that any person or persons may then appear and shew [*sic*] cause why the prayer thereof may not be granted." The *New Hampshire Gazette* published the petition July 15, 1780, but added a disclaimer that it was printed for their readers' "amusement." The General Assembly postponed the hearing they had scheduled and nothing more was done.

In the year 2013, New Hampshire State Senator Martha Fuller Clark of Portsmouth presented a bill to the legislature granting freedom posthumously to the twenty men who signed the petition. It passed both houses unanimously. Governor Maggie Hassan signed the bill into law on June 7, 2013, in Portsmouth, stating amid cheers that it corrected a "centuries-overdue wrong." Ironically again, there was no mention of the many other Black people across New Hampshire in 1779 who also were known by "the name of slave" but could not produce a petition.

Signers of the Petition in 1779

> Nero Brewster
> Will Clarkson
> Garrett Colton
> Peter Frost
> Zebulon Gardner
> Ceaser Gerrish*
> Seneca Hall
> Cipio Hubbard
> Winsor Moffat
> Cato Newmarch
> Jack Odiorne*
> Pharaoh Roberts
> Romeo Rindge *
> Quam Sherburne
> Pharaoh Shores*
> Kittindge Tuckerman

Cato Warner
Peter Warner*
Samuel Wentworth
Prince Whipple*

*There is documentation that shows these six men gained freedom in their lifetime after the petition was written. The status of the other men is unknown.

Read the Petition at www.trinityhistory.org/AmH/SlavesNH1779. pdf

---

Collect Day 22 ❦ The 1779 Petition for Freedom

Lord, you have created every person in your image, making each a unique and beloved child. Forgive the sin of those who came before us, not only denying that enslaved people are human, but ridiculing their demand that they be recognized as equal children of God. As we repent our own blindness to the value of others, guide us to an amendment of life, so that your Kingdom may thrive throughout our land. In the name of Christ Jesus, who died for the sake of all humanity. Amen.

Day 23
Andover, NH

Richard Potter

(1783 – 1835)
J. Dennis Robinson

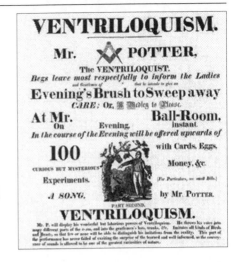

*L*EGEND SAYS that Richard
Potter, America's first
native-born stage magician,
could climb into one end of
a solid log and exit from the other end. He once made a rooster
pull a heavy load of hay up a steep hill. According to a man
from Andover, NH, where Potter once owned a farm, dozens of
witnesses standing in an open field saw Potter toss a ball of yarn
into the air, then he and his wife, Sally, climbed up the dangling
string into the sky and disappeared.

Those miraculous events never happened, of course. Nor was Potter
the illegitimate son of Benjamin Franklin and his African servant.
Potter was born in Hopkinton, Massachusetts, to an enslaved
woman from Guinea who had been sold at auction on a Boston
pier. His father was a White man, repeatedly in trouble, who was
banned from his church for "making attempts on the chastity" of at
least six women.

Richard Potter traveled to Europe as a teenager and there was
likely apprenticed to a famous Italian acrobat and tightrope artist
or "wire dancer." By 1803 Potter was working as a "polite waiter"
at the Portsmouth Hotel near present-day Prescott Park in
Portsmouth, New Hampshire. He likely performed "a number of
feats on the rope, with the balance pole." After touring with a pair
of Scottish-born magicians and ventriloquists, Potter struck out
on his own. He married Sally Harris, a petite young singer who,

despite most reports, was not a full-blooded Penobscot Indian.

We can hardly imagine the hard life of an itinerant African American performer in an age before trains and electricity, before emancipation, and largely without formal theaters to perform in. Yet Potter's celebrity exploded. A master of misdirection, his singular goal was to distract audiences from their toilsome lives. His advertising handbills offered "to give an evening's brush to sweep away care."

He could make a playing card vanish and reappear across the room, catch a bullet on the point of a sword, or break and recreate a gold ring. His balancing skills involved long-stemmed clay pipes, plates, swords, glasses, keys, tables and chairs, plus a variety of silverware. Witnesses claimed he could step into a blazing oven with a joint of raw meat and emerge with it fully cooked. But it was Potter's ability to throw his voice that drew the greatest praise. His ventriloquism filled the hall with invisible birds, animals, beckoning children, and crying babies.

All but forgotten by history, Richard Potter, America's first native-born magician and first Black celebrity, is the subject of a rich new biography by scholar John A. Hodgson. Potter's final years turned tragic as racism raged in America. His once expansive farm at Potter's Place near Andover, NH, is gone, but his grave, a roadside plaque and now a stirring new biography keep his magical story alive.

Collect Day 23 ☙ Richard Potter

Loving father, who has delighted in creating a world of wonder for your children: we thank you for the witness of Richard Potter, who used his gifts as entertainer to bring joy throughout his life. Help us to follow in his example, doing our best to use our own God given talents to bring true pleasure to others; through Christ our Lord. Amen.

Day 24
Portsmouth, NH

Esther Whipple Mullinaux

(1785 – 1868)
Angela Matthews

*I*N 1827 ESTHER MULLINAUX, the daughter of Prince and Dinah Whipple, was living on the street where she had grown up and where her widowed mother still conducted the local school for Black children. By the 1830s their High Street home was deemed unsafe for the two women alone. In consideration of Dinah wanting to continue to live within walking distance of her church, the women moved into a house on Pleasant Street that was generously provided by the family that formerly enslaved Prince. Like her parents and siblings, Esther also was a member of North Church in Portsmouth. The church baptized the Black family's children, officiated at their marriages, even assisted with cash gifts during Dinah's final two winters, then provided for her burial in 1846.

Esther married a mariner, William Mullinaux, in 1801. Their children were William Prince, Anna, Elizabeth, Richard and Horace William. In 1815 Esther's husband disappeared, thought to be lost at sea, and she remarried. This, however, created a controversy which led to the marriage being declared unlawful by the church. Esther was admonished and in 1817, according to customary practices of that time; her public confession of "shame and confusion of face" was transcribed into the North Church record book.

Her persistence and tenacity over the years allowed Esther, like other Blacks in an often-hostile world, to survive and even thrive. Supplementing steady work as a laundress with housekeeping, sewing and childcare, by 1851 Esther was able to purchase a house at auction.

Upon her death in 1868, Esther's will stipulated that North Church was to receive the proceeds of her estate for the purpose of foreign and home missionary work. In particular, she asked that her bequest be used for the home mission projects sponsored by both North and South churches in support of schools and other services for newly freed African Americans. Her estate was valued at just over $300, the house having appreciated over fourteen years from a value of $200. Esther Mullinaux is buried in a marked grave near her parents in North Cemetery.

Collect Day 24 ❦ Esther Whipple Mullinaux

O God of Wisdom, today we remember Esther, daughter of a slave, faithful church member and laborer. Despite losing her husband and being shamed by the church, Esther persisted. Her tenacity and hard work enabled her to thrive, and even after her death she had the means to support the education of newly freed slaves. We ask that we may have her strength, when we feel ashamed, to keep working. We ask that we find the means to thrive, and that our hearts will be as dedicated to generous mission work as was Esther's. We give thanks for this woman of great strength, and we rejoice that she made a difference to others in life and in death. We offer these prayers in the name of Jesus, who also suffered shame, who lived his life for others, and whose death brings us all new life. Amen.

Day 25
Portsmouth, NH

Cyrus / Siras DeBruce

Angela Matthews

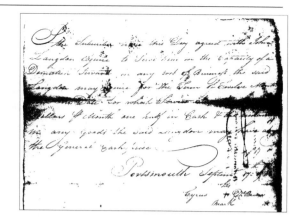

*S*IRAS DeBruce escaped from the family now claiming ownership of him, believing his previous owner, Isaac Levy, had provided for Siras to be freed upon Levy's death in 1777. Instead, Levy's daughter Henrietta and her husband, Mathias Williamson, Jr. chose not to honor that understanding because no signed document stating Levy's intention could be found.

Bruce sought refuge with British troops in New York where he remained until he came into the employment with Gov. John Langdon of Portsmouth. It is unclear where and when Bruce and Langdon met but it is clear that Langdon was impressed. Bruce entered into a voluntary agreement Sept. 17, 1783, to work for Langdon for one year, for $6 a month, doing "any sort of business the said Langdon may require." Bruce signed the contract with his X and was compensated in food, shelter and clothing as well as the monthly stipend.

According to oral tradition and an account of *Brewster's Rambles* (1856) in the *Portsmouth Freeman's Journal,*

> There could scarcely be found in Portsmouth, not excepting the Governor himself, one who dressed more elegantly or exhibited a more gentlemanly appearance. His heavy gold chain and seals, his fine black or blue broadcloth coat and small clothes, his silk stocking and silver-buckled shoes, his

ruffles and carefully plaited linen, are well remembered by many.

When George Washington visited Portsmouth on his tour of the country following his inauguration in 1789, Bruce would have been elegant in appearance and manners when he greeted the new country's first President at the door of John Langdon's mansion.

On May 4, 1785, Siras married Flora, an African woman who had formerly been the property of tavern owner James Stoodley and valued in his estate at £100. Flora and Siras lived in a small brick building directly behind the Langdon house. Bruce continued as Langdon's trusted employee for fourteen years and may have been among those servants designated to receive bequests ranging from $50 to $200 upon Langdon's death. This generosity by Langdon, the abolitionist, might have been an act of conscience by this abolitionist for his family accumulating wealth through the Colonial-era slavery.

Collect Day 25 ⚜ Cyrus /Siras DeBruce

O God who clothes the lilies, we give you thanks for the life of Siras DeBruce. We have learned that he was a man of bravery, who spent his life working for other men. We give special thanks for his sense of style and his elegant appearance, even as a servant. We thank you for his courage to stand out. We thank you for his pride and individuality. We pray that all of us may have the conviction to let our light shine and not hide in the shadows. We ask this in the name of our Creator, our Redeemer and our Sanctifier. Amen.

Betsey Due Razee

(1794 – 1836)
Eric Aldrich

PART OF OBSERVING LENT is repenting for our sins. As difficult as that may be for some of us, repenting was a particular challenge for Betsey Due Razee. Born into a mixed-race family in Hancock, New Hampshire, in 1790, Betsey spent two years of her life in the mid-1820s arguing with Rev. Archibald Burgess and a church committee investigating her marriage difficulties.

Within his first six months as pastor of the Hancock Church of Christ, Rev. Burgess in 1823 led his first formal inquiry of discipline for the church. The Due family, identified in US censuses as free people of color, were members of the church. Burgess's predecessor, Rev. Reed Paige, led a discipline inquiry into Betsey's mother in 1794. Hannah Due was alleged to have been married to another man when she had an adulterous relationship with her current husband, James Due.

Jump ahead to 1823, when Rev. Burgess's church appointed a committee to "inquire and adjust if possible the difficulties between Mr. (Richard) Razee and his wife (Betsey), a member of this church."

In 1824, the church committee reported that Richard left his wife and children two years prior but was now willing "to return to his duty and live in peace and harmony with his wife, making confession to the church and to her, provided that she would meet him in similar terms."

An Unforgiving Temper of Mind

Betsey would have none of it. The church reported that "she utterly refused to receive him as a husband." That was in March 1824, the moment that Rev. Burgess and his church committee suspended their attention to Richard Razee's abandonment of his family and focused instead on Betsey. Among the church's charges against Betsey were that she refused "to be reconciled to her husband, except upon unreasonable terms," namely that he "manifest that he was a Christian by at least one year's life of holiness."

Over months of humiliating hearings before the church, Betsey stood her ground, refusing to repent or to have her husband back. Burgess wrote in the church records that Betsey manifested "an implacable disposition, an unforgiving temper of mind and unchristian spirit." At Betsey's suggestion, the church convened a council of pastors from neighboring towns to consider the matter. After a day-long trial in June 1825, the council ruled against Betsey, adding that she designed to entice her husband "into the crime of adultery, with a view to facilitate separation."

Despite her angry disagreement with the ruling and the church's position, Betsey prepared a confession. "I have sinned and now wish to make the satisfaction which the gospel requires," Betsey's letter reads. At length in her letter Betsey repented her sins and implored the church for forgiveness.

Confessions Rejected

But the church rejected Betsey's repentance. "Mrs. Razee refused to give any answers," according to Burgess's notes. "And her appearance was highly dissatisfactory to the church as manifesting an impenitent and unchristian spirit." More church letters admonishing her followed. By early 1826, Betsey had prepared a second letter of confession. The church rejected that confession, too, noting that she neglected to attend meetings when her case was under consideration.

In May 1826 the church excommunicated Betsey, along with her husband, Richard Razee, in absentia. By then, Richard Razee had long left his wife and children for a new life in New York state. Betsey was thirty-six, with three surviving children, and had endured more than two dozen meetings in the case over the past two years.

Betsey Due Razee's story was one of many dramas that played out in this town in the decades before the Civil War. Her determination to stand up against the church's pious leaders are gleaned in the thin scraps of remaining archives, but absent from the history books. Her complex story holds many lingering riddles, touched by shades of skin color, a family's heritage and the sometimes-interrupted arc of repentance.

Collect Day 26 ☙ Betsey Due Razee

God of forgiveness, whose will it is always to have mercy, we remember before you Betsey Due Razee, about whom we know so little. We do know that she was investigated, humiliated and singled out by her church for the misdeeds of her husband. And we know that she had the courage to stand her ground, alone, until she had no choice, and still was mistreated. We ask your forgiveness for the sins of your church, past and present. We ask that we have our eyes opened when we judge needlessly or unfairly. We pray for the many, like Betsey, whom the church has persecuted. Let Betsey's story convict us when we show no understanding or mercy. May we be humble enough to give thanks for her convictions and her steadfastness. In Jesus' name we pray. Amen.

Day 27
Henniker, NH

Nancy Gardner Prince

(1799 – c. 1856)
Edith Butler

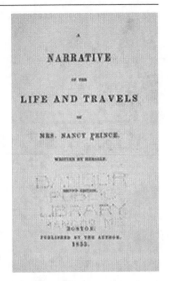

A *Black Woman's Odyssey Through
Russia and Jamaica: The Narrative
of Nancy Prince*, first published in 1850, is
one of the few surviving autobiographical
accounts by a free Black woman in the
pre-Civil War North. Nancy Gardner Prince's life ranges from her
birth in Newburyport, Massachusetts, to the palace of a Russian
Czar, to Jamaica at its turbulent end of slavery.

Nancy's family was among about 6,500 free African Americans
living in Massachusetts. Thus, Nancy grew up among a variety
of cultures. Some of her family were servants to well-to-do New
Englanders, which brought them in contact with the manners
and culture of prosperous and learned Whites. At home, her
grandfather and her mother's third husband — both "stolen from
Africa" — told the children proud tales of life there. And Nancy
and her siblings were entertained with stories of the seafaring life
— a common occupation among free African American men.

Her father, Thomas Gardner, a freeman, was a seaman from
Nantucket who died when Nancy was three months old. Her
mother was the daughter of slaves, had a Native American
grandmother and married several times. Always on the brink of
poverty, the death of Nancy's second stepfather was an economic
disaster that contributed to her mother's physical and emotional
breakdown. Nancy and her six younger siblings, all under age
fourteen, worked tirelessly — not just doing the laundry, cooking

and cleaning, but also catching and selling fish and picking and selling berries — to help support the family. Nancy wrote that she and her siblings stayed with their mother "until every resource [was] exhausted." Eventually, the children were placed in homes as servants for White families, except for Nancy's younger brother who went to sea.

Nancy Gardner's life changes dramatically again when she married Nero Prince in 1824. Her narrative gives no details of how they met or their courtship. Mr. Prince arrives from Russia on Feb. 15, 1824. They marry, and on April 14 they embark for Russia where Nero worked as a footman at the court of Czar Alexander.

Mrs. Prince covers vividly the dramatic events she witnessed while her husband served in the Czar's court. She wrote that she started a children's clothing business, started an orphanage and learned Russian and some French. When Nancy's health began to decline in 1833 she returned to America. Her husband was to follow but died in Russia.

In Boston, Nancy used her skills as a seamstress to start a business. She also participated in activities of the bi-racial Boston Female Anti-Slavery Society and gave public lectures about her travels and her life in Russia. In 1840 and 1842 Nancy decided to go to Jamaica to help establish schools and spiritual programs for freed children. Unfortunately, the Jamaican apprentice plan started breaking down, leading to a breakdown of order and a certain amount for chaos for those like Mrs. Prince, coming to establish programs. What Mrs. Prince described as "deceitful" and "mercenary" missionaries flooded the island and began to make her work difficult and dangerous. She left Jamaica. Nevertheless, despite the disappointing outcome of her Jamaica project and a health-breaking and perilous trip home, she was committed to anti-slavery work.

Back in Boston, she fell on hard times, living on the kindness of friends. But not wanting to be a burden, she decided to write her memoirs, hoping to support herself at least in part from the sales. The book was published in 1850, a second edition in 1853, followed by a third in 1856. Her narratives provide vivid evocative, eyewitness accounts of the unique experiences of this intrepid, African American woman. Nothing is yet known of the circumstances of Nancy Prince's death.

Collect Day 27 ❦ Nancy Gardner Prince

O Word which became flesh and dwelt among us: we lift up today Nancy Gardner Prince, author, courageous educator, protector of orphans, business woman and world traveler who proudly shared her story and heritage in brilliant clarity; may we be inspired by her tireless efforts to help those in need regardless of their heritage so that all division may be erased from your beautiful world; this we ask in the Name of him who call us all God's children, Jesus Christ our Lord. Amen

Day 28
Pittsfield, NH

Frederick Douglass in New Hampshire

(c. 1818 – 1895)

J. Dennis Robinson

*I*N THE FINAL version of his autobiography, published not long before his death in 1895, Frederick Douglass recalled an early visit to New Hampshire. Now America's best-known abolitionist, Douglass was just twenty-five during his first encounter with citizens of the Granite State. Twenty-one of those years had been spent enslaved.

He bore on his back the marks of the lash, and he likely revealed this fact to his White audience in Pittsfield, NH, in 1842. He knew White audiences did not want to hear the horrific details of life as a slave, but he told them all the same.

"I'm afraid you do not understand the awful character of these lashes," Douglass said politely. He explained how an enslaved man could be stripped naked, tied to a tree or post and — for the smallest of infractions — lashed with a knotted whip almost to the bone.

A Black woman who taught her child to read was hanged, he said. There were seventy-one crimes for which a Black could be executed, Douglass noted, yet only three capital crimes for Whites. As he spoke to the Pittsfield congregation, Douglass himself was a fugitive and still enslaved. He had escaped his Maryland owner to marry a free Black woman named Anne Murray.

During a morning intermission in the Pittsfield service, no one in the congregation spoke to Douglass. At lunch no one spoke to him or offered him a meal. Rejected from a local hotel, cold, hungry and despondent, Douglass sat in a small cemetery. Only the New Hampshire dead, Douglass wrote, welcomed him.

America was in the thick of its gruesome Civil War when Douglass arrived in Portsmouth two decades later March 15, 1862. His own sons were soldiers. He spoke this time at the 1,000-seat Portsmouth Lyceum in a converted church known as The Temple on the site of today's Music Hall. By this time Douglass was a free man, well known for his fiery impassioned rhetoric, as publisher of the anti-slavery *North Star* newspaper, and as a confidante of President Abraham Lincoln.

This time the local papers trumpeted Douglass' arrival. A display ad in the *Portsmouth Daily Morning Chronicle* announced the evening lecture by "The Eloquent Champion of Freedom." Slavery, like indentured servitude, Douglass reminded his many nineteenth-century audiences, was initially about cheap labor, not race. Many nations and races practiced slavery, he explained. But in America, as the nation evolved, successful businessmen became addicted to slavery, even as slavery became identified with skin color. The addiction to criminally cheap labor was hard to break, and as history shows us every day, the scars of racism have yet to heal.

Collect Day 28 ⚓ Frederick Douglass In
New Hampshire

Almighty God, we bless your Name for the witness of Frederick Douglass, whose impassioned and reasonable speech moved the hearts of people to a deeper obedience to Christ even as was "warned out" of many towns in New Hampshire: Strengthen us also to speak on behalf of those in captivity and tribulation, continuing in the Word of Jesus Christ our Liberator; who with you and the Holy Spirit dwells in glory everlasting. Amen

Oliver Cromwell Gilbert

(c. 1828 – 1912)
Jody Fernald

*N*O TUNNELS, secret rooms or painted chimneys appeared in Oliver Cromwell Gilbert's description of his journey in 1852 from slavery in Maryland to the home of the Cartland family in Lee, New Hampshire.

Gilbert appeared at the Cartland homestead on a snowy April night, bearing a letter of introduction from abolitionist William Lloyd Garrison of Boston. The members of The Boston Vigilance Committee, both Black and White playing different roles, had housed and employed Gilbert during his stay in Boston at a time when slaveholders came looking to recover their property under the protection of the second Fugitive Slave Act. His story reveals much about the journey many took to escape a life of enslavement and fight for a life in freedom.

Oliver Gilbert was born into slavery on Maryland's western shore around 1828. He had served primarily as a household servant and escaped in 1848 with a group of young men including some of his siblings. Gilbert left a record of his journey detailing the help he received from Quakers, free Blacks and others through Pennsylvania, New York, New Jersey and Boston. While in Boston, Garrison and others helped him reconnect with one of his sisters who also had escaped from slavery.

Gilbert was sent to the Quaker Cartland family in Lee. The Cartlands were no ordinary rural farmers. They were educators and political and social activists who worked across the Northeast, including Pennsylvania and New York. While in Lee, Gilbert lectured to the students of the Cartlands' Quaker school, as well as to sympathetic local residents. He did not hide in the basement although he certainly was not considered a social or intellectual equal. His story was compelling and his oratorical and musical talents made him an effective teacher about the evils of slavery. But Lee lacked a community of Black people of similar experiences, so Gilbert moved back to Boston when it appeared safe to do so.

Gilbert went on to lecture throughout the Northeast, as well as perform with his Gilbert Family Singers. He moved to New York where he ran the Gilbert House hotel in Saratoga Springs in a community of free and formerly enslaved Blacks. Gilbert took his wife and children to the 1876 exposition in a Philadelphia and was so impressed that the family moved there shortly thereafter. He continued to correspond and visit with the Cartlands and their descendants and remained forever grateful for the assistance they gave him.

Gilbert never went to Canada although that was his original intention. Instead, he found supportive communities among his people and continued to work for their benefit. He died in Philadelphia with little financial resources, but he had contributed immensely to expanding later knowledge of those who had survived their enslavement and the ways in which they navigated the difficulties of a culture steeped in racial prejudice.

For more details on Oliver Gilbert's life see:
Fernald, Jody "In Slavery and In Freedom: Oliver C. Gilbert and Edwin S. Warfield." *Maryland Historical Magazine*, Summer 2011, p141–161.
Fernald, Jody and Gilbert, Stephanie, "Oliver Cromwell Gilbert: A Life" (2014). University Library Scholarship. Paper 75.

Collect Day 29 ❦ Oliver Cromwell Gilbert

O God of Abraham, Isaac and Jacob who called your people out of bondage and death into life and freedom: we lift up today Oliver Cromwell Gilbert who bravely escaped the evils of slavery in America to begin a new life as an educator, musician, husband and father; may we like those who helped Oliver to find safety to pursue his courageous battle against racism also never waiver in our responsibility to speak out against all forms of oppression; this we ask in the Name of Jesus Christ who calls us all from death to life. Amen

Day 30
Milford, NH

Harriet Wilson

(1825 – 1900)
David H. Watters

*H*ARRIET E. (HATTIE) ADAMS was
born in Milford in 1825. Her
father, Joshua Green, was an African
American, and her mother, Margaret Adams or Smith, was White.
After her father's death, Harriet was abandoned by her mother at
the home of Nehemiah Hayward Jr. and Rebecca S. Hutchinson
Hayward. She attended the local district school for three years,
1832–34. She was probably indentured as a servant, and she
remained in the Hayward household until turning eighteen in
1843. She returned to the house during an illness later in 1846.

During these years, she would have been aware of the growing
abolitionist sentiment in town, led by the Hutchinson Family
Singers and Parker Pillsbury of Milford, climaxing in a massive
rally in January 1843 attended by all the great abolitionists of the
day: William Lloyd Garrison, Wendell Phillips, Parker Pillsbury,
Nathan P. Rogers, C.L. Remond, Abby Kelley, Stephen S. Foster,
George Latimer, and Frederick Douglass.

For several years in the late 1840s and 1850s, Wilson alternated
between employment in Milford and probably Ware or Worcester
in Massachusetts, and periods as a pauper in New Hampshire at
the Hillsborough County Poor Farm or boarding with Milford
families. In Ware or Worcester, she improved her education
and aspired to write, and she met Thomas Wilson, a professed
fugitive slave and a mariner, whom she married in 1851. Their
child, George Mason Wilson, was born in 1852. His absence at

sea and then the death of Thomas in 1853, left Wilson and their son impoverished. Wilson made and sold hair products in the late 1850s and turned to authorship, publishing *Our Nig: Sketches from the Life of a Free Black in 1859*, in an attempt to support her son. But he died in 1860.

Wilson is considered the first African American woman — as well as the first African American of any gender — to publish a novel in the US. As the research of Gates, White, Ellis, Foreman, and Pitts show, Wilson's novel *Our Nig*, closely follows Wilson's life, detailing the life and suffering of Frado, a mixed-race child who, abandoned by her mother, becomes a servant for a White family in the free North. Members of the novel's Bellmont family have been identified as the Hayward and Hutchinson families of Milford. Other Milford people and individuals in other towns in which Frado/Wilson resided have also been identified, permitting readers to ascertain the veracity of her story and the artistry by which she transformed it into a novel.

Wilson became involved in the spiritualist movement during the 1860s, and for the rest of her life gained fame as a spiritualist medium and "doctor." Spiritualists were at the forefront of New England reform movements — from abolitionism, women's rights, and temperance to educational and economic reform.

Early in 1883, Wilson opened a new Sunday school for the children of "the liberal minded" in the parlors of members of the Ladies Aid Societies in Boston at a time when Black woman teaching White children in a private school such as Wilson's was still quite extraordinary.

Wilson later married a White apothecary, John Gallatin Robinson, but this marriage did not last. Until the late 1890s, Wilson is listed in spiritualist publications and Boston city directories as a trance reader and lecturer. Her novel had long since disappeared from view, but she was celebrated and remembered at her death in 1900 as a spiritualist.

Harriet Wilson, who began her life as an indentured servant in the 1830s on a Milford farm, ended up writing an important piece of American literature. *Our Nig* is recognized for what it is: a remarkable literary achievement that offers a unique and important view of a turbulent — and often ugly — time in America's past.

Collect Day 30 🕯 Harriet Wilson

O God, present to us in the embrace of the Holy Spirit: we remember today Harriett Wilson, daughter of Milford, New Hampshire and first African American novelist; we thank you for her voice, for her perseverance through hardship and for her exploration of the spirits that deepened her understanding of all that is seen and unseen in your creation; may we find in her heroic story the immeasurable value of all human life and repent of any trace of bigotry and racism that lurks in our souls; through Jesus Christ our Lord we pray. Amen

Day 31
Canaan, NH

Noyes Academy

(1835)
JerriAnne Boggis

*I*N 1835 A GROUP of New Hampshire abolitionists opened Noyes Academy, the first racially integrated and coeducational school, based on the idea that women and Blacks had the same rights as White males to a formal education. At the time, although many cities offered some form of segregated schooling for Black children, a classical education was inaccessible to African Americans.

Evidence suggests that fourteen of the roughly forty students, mainly teenagers, in Noyes Academy's first and only class, were African Americans, including at least one Black woman, Julia Williams. Traveling under treacherous and hostile conditions, they came from all over the Northeast to take advantage of this opportunity.

Within months of its opening, anti-abolitionists in Canaan and neighboring towns, including Hanover, Dorchester and Enfield, began agitating for the town to close the school. A campaign to discredit school officials and cultivate fear over the possibility of interracial marriage and racial mixing soon followed.

In August of 1835, hundreds of men from Canaan and surrounding towns, launched an assault on the school. They arrived with ninety oxen, ropes and chains. It would take several days, but eventually, working in shifts, they physically dragged the schoolhouse off its foundation and demolished it. After destroying the school, the mob threatened the students and the people sheltering them by firing cannons at the homes. The students had to be smuggled out of town under cover of night.

Thus, New Hampshire's brief experiment in educational equality ended. However, the school launched the careers of several extraordinary African-American leaders, including Alexander Crummell and Henry Highland Garnet.

After he escaped from Canaan, Alexander Crummell continued his education in New York where he was forced to study privately after being denied admittance to the General Theological Seminary of the Episcopal Church because of his race. Nonetheless, at the age of twenty-five, he became an Episcopalian minister and went on to graduate from Queens' College in England. Crummell founded St. Luke's Episcopal Church in Washington, DC and organized a group now known as the Union of Black Episcopalians to fight racial discrimination in the church. Crummell, who would become a major influence on innumerable Black leaders, including DuBois, Dunbar and Garvey, died in Point Pleasant, New Jersey in 1898.

Henry Highland Garnet became prominent nationally when he delivered a speech entitled "Call to Rebellion," urging enslaved people to rise up against their owners and claim their own freedom. He became the pastor of the Fifteenth Street Presbyterian Church in Washington D.C. and he was the first African American to make a speech in the Capitol Building. Garnet was appointed ambassador to Liberia by President James A. Garfield in December 1881 and he died there on February 13, 1882, barely two months after his arrival.

Collect Day 31 🦌 Noyes Academy

O God, Ancient Heart of Love who instills us with the Divine Spark of Grace: we thank you for the courageous witness of abolitionists who built Noyes Academy for all, for Julia Williams who risked her life to be educated, for the Rev. Alexander Crummell who dared to fight against segregation within the church, and for the Rev. Henry Highland Garnet who inspired rebellion against evil. May the examples of their faith be an inspiration for all of us to become like them, the Word made Flesh; in Jesus' name we pray, the rock of our salvation. Amen

Nellie Brown Mitchell

(1845 – 1924)
Darryl Glenn Nettles

*N*ELLIE BROWN MITCHELL, a Dover native, was a prominent African American opera singer during the 1850s and 1860s. Her stage career lasted ten years, during which she formed her own company, the Nellie Brown Mitchell Concert Company.

Nellie Brown was born in 1845. While in Dover, she studied with Caroline Bracket, who encouraged her to pursue a professional vocal career. She began in 1865 at the Free-Will Baptist Church, an Anglo-American Church. Brown was the soprano soloist. Service to the church would prove to be a distinct part of her musical career.

In 1872 she left Free-Will Baptist Church to serve as soloist at Grace Church in Haverhill, Massachusetts. Brown studied voice with Mrs. J. Rametti and Professor O'Neill, returning to Dover in 1876. Brown studied at the New England Conservatory and the School of Vocal Arts. She received her diploma in 1879, then she served as musical director at the Bloomfield Street Church in Boston until 1886.

Nellie Brown had given a series of successful recitals in Boston and made her New York debut at Steinway Hall by 1874. She debuted in Philadelphia in 1882 and was a "prima donna soprano" with James Bergen's Star Concerts until 1885. Flora Batson replaced her when prior concert obligations in the South prevented her from attending a concert in Providence, Rhode Island. She resigned her

Bloomfield church position to devote her time to her concert career and her newly formed Nellie Brown Mitchell Concert Company, which included her sister, soprano Ednah B. Brown. Nellie's husband was Lt. Charles L. Mitchell, a member of the 55th Massachusetts Negro Regiment.

During the 1880s and into the 1890s Nellie Brown Mitchell reached the peak of her concert career, touring the East Coast and Midwest. Her reputation won her great admiration from colleagues and critics. She was considered by many to be the greatest African American singer of her time and the only rival of Marie Selika Williams, first Black artist to perform at the White House.

For many summers Nellie Mitchell taught at the Hedding Chautauqua Summer School in East Epping, New Hampshire. In the 1890s she retired from the concert stage and devoted her time to private teaching, advertising that she taught the Guilmette Method of vocal technique. She died in Boston in January 1924.

Adapted from an article reproduced with permission from the Dover Public Library.

Collect Day 32 ☙ Nellie Brown Mitchell

O God, the source of the blessed gifts we receive: today we remember Nellie Brown Mitchell and her gift of a beautiful singing voice, which she shared with the world, in worship of You, and by teaching others; may she be a reminder to us to appreciate and use the precious gifts we have received from You; through Jesus Christ our Lord, who lives and reigns with you and the Holy Spirit, one God, now and forever. Amen

Day 33
Dover, NH

Lydia Chesley Dixon & James Dixon

Jody Fernald

HERE IS no known existing image of Lydia Dixon of
Dover. She would have become lost to the history of New
Hampshire had she not joined an antislavery organization in Dover
— the records of which were preserved, and had her father not left
military and probate records of his life.

Lydia's father, Corydon Chesley, was born into slavery in New
Hampshire. He died in 1831 at age ninety-one, having lived over
fifty years after he purchased his freedom from the Chesley family.
Records of Lydia and her sister Abigail allow us to trace the lives of
the next generation after slavery in New Hampshire.

Four years after her father's death, Lydia, a member of the First
Church of Dover, appeared as a member of the Ladies' Antislavery
Society of Dover under the leadership of Rev. David Root. Lydia,
a woman of mixed race and daughter of a man born into slavery,
knew far better than her sister members the legacy of slavery.

Dover's population of color at the time numbered fifteen,
including children. Lydia, like most free Blacks at the time, lived a
subordinate status both in the antislavery organization and in the
community. Her third husband, James Dixon, was a Black barber
from Jamaica who first appeared in Portsmouth records c. 1830.
James and his brother-in-law were both professional barbers at the

New Hampshire Hotel, an occupation common among free Blacks in the area.

Lydia joined the church in 1830 and her husband, James, joined in 1831, although records indicate James was not committed to the church and was willingly excommunicated for nonattendance in 1842. Church records labeled James as a Negro while no race had been indicated for Lydia who had connections to several local families. James moved his barbershop to the waterfront of Dover in 1834 where he may have come into contact with others from Jamaica or those escaping slavery through maritime routes. Shipping traffic on the Cocheco River was brisk in the early nineteenth century since many of Dover's ship owners also lived and worked in Portsmouth.

The advent of a management class in Dover's mills brought new class distinctions and changes in the goals and composition of the original antislavery organization. Lydia became disenfranchised and moved with other members of the artisan class to establish the Belknap Church of Dover, named after the eighteenth-century clergyman Jeremy Belknap who authorized her father's manumission papers in 1778. Founding members indicated their dissatisfaction with a community in which "irreligion and vice so prevail."

In 1858, Lydia Dixon, a widow, left a will detailing how she would continue to care for the women in her life. She left her sister, Abigail Moore, wife of Dover's Black barber William Moore, two rooms in her house where she was residing at the time. She left the rest of her estate to her niece, Elizabeth Fowler, wife of Samuel Fowler Jr. of Malden, Massachusetts, and to Elizabeth James ("commonly called Elizabeth Dixon") whom she had raised. Lydia died in 1868 after a life spent actively opposing slavery and caring for the members of her immediate family.

For more information on Lydia Dixon, see:
Fernald, Jody R. "Radical Reform in Public Sentiment: Lydia

Dixon and the Dover, New Hampshire Ladies' Antislavery Society," Dublin Seminar for New England Folklife: Annual Proceedings 2003. Boston University Scholarly Publications, 2005. p.92–101.

Collect Day 33 ❦ Lydia Chesley Dixon & James Dixon

Holy God, in whose Son is revealed in the beauty and breadth of the human family; Strengthen and sustain us, just as you did for your servants Lydia & James. Give us the courage to persevere in the face of injustice, oppression and all that enslaves and seeks to make invisible the glory of your Creation; and pray that we, through their worthy example, may receive the inspiration of your Holy Spirit to protect and gather all that seek safety and freedom through our brother, Jesus Christ; who with you and the Holy Spirit lives and reigns, one God now and forever. Amen

Day 34
Weare & Mont Vernon, NH

Caesar Parker

Reginald Pitts

*T*HE STORIES of early African American residents survive only through anecdotes. This is true of Caesar Parker, originally from Methuen, Massachusetts, and later of Weare, New Hampshire. Although a longtime resident of Mont Vernon, for a time Parker lived in Milford. Parker is a good example of the clown-character typical of White descriptions of free African Americans in antebellum accounts.

In this case, the source of Parker's portrait is native son John Hutchinson of the famous antislavery Hutchinson Singers. According to Hutchinson, Parker was a town "character," remembered as "Black as the ace of spades." He was "a tall, well-proportioned, athletic, uneducated but witty African" who worked on farms in Milford and Amherst.

Hutchinson recalls that Parker was "quite conspicuous on public occasions, like trainings, musters, and holidays, with the b'hoys, who were fond of scuffling and wrestling. He was always brought into the ring under the influence of a glass or two, which was freely furnished him, was sufficiently bold and sprightly, and could bring down, to the amusement of all, almost any of those selected to scuffle or wrestle." In fact, Parker appears in two comedic stories recounted by John Hutchinson.

In the first, a young White girl, jilted by her lover, is heard to sigh that she would marry the first man that asked her. "Some wag," writes Hutchinson, goes up to Parker, tells him that "Miss So-and-So is very fond of you," and that if he hastens to her and proposes marriage, she would accept. Consequently, this colored man dressed himself in his best overalls, repaired to the house, and boldly made his proposition; and to his great delight the lady agreed that he should be her suitor. Subsequently they married, and the result was that instead of one Black man in our neighborhood, there soon grew up five boys and two girls of a lighter hue." The second story shows Parker out trapping for beaver along the banks of the Souhegan River. It describes his consternation when he found out someone placed a dead house cat in his trap.

In addition to such patronizing anecdotes, public records show that Caesar Parker and Margaret Spear of New Ipswich, New Hampshire, married around 1800 and had five boys and two girls. Although they were remembered as "athletic and dexterous" and "fond of music," the boys felt keenly the sting of being different in homogeneous Milford. While they were able to attend the district schools, there "was observable a notable reservation and withdrawing from the common plays and sports of the children." Later, one of the sons, described as "a very agreeable, pleasant man, speaking familiarly of his relation and his condition, said he would suffer to be skinned alive if he could rid himself of his color."

Collect Day 34 ☙ Caesar Parker

O loving and gracious God, who created each and every one of us with Your unlimited Love: we lift up your servant Caesar Parker who was bold and unafraid to face a new challenge and his mixed-race children who suffered prejudice for being seen as different; Help us to see each other in the same loving light in which You created us that we love and embrace all humankind; through Jesus Christ our Lord, who lives and reigns with you and the Holy Spirit, one God, now and forever. Amen.

Day 35
Durham, NH

Elizabeth Ann Virgil

(? – 1991)
Angela Matthews

*O*N MAY 26, 1926, Portsmouth's Elizabeth Ann Virgil became the first African American to graduate from the University of New Hampshire, where she majored in home economics and was active in several music clubs including the Treble Clefs, a group she helped to found.

White social conventions at the time prohibited Elizabeth from teaching in New Hampshire and necessitated her moving to the South to teach in segregated schools in Virginia and Maryland. She was an exceptional teacher and was sent by her school district for advanced courses at Columbia Teachers College. In the late 1930s she gave up teaching and returned to Portsmouth to care for her mother. She held various positions with small local businesses as well as clerk-typist in the Programming Department at Portsmouth Naval Shipyard. In 1951 she took a job as secretary in the Soil Conservation Department of UNH where she worked for twenty-two years until her retirement in 1973.

Elizabeth Virgil's portrait hangs near the entrance to the Dimond Library. Unveiled at a reception in 1991, the painting by Grant Drumheller depicts her beloved piano and surrounds her serene presence with roses and lilacs. The university bestowed the honor in recognition of "the barriers she had overcome and the trail she had blazed as the first Black woman to graduate from the institution."

Miss Virgil, as she was known by all, established a scholarship fund in honor of her mother, Alberta Curry Virgil, who was born the daughter of a former slave. "She encouraged us on so many impossible things because she believed that God was with us," said Miss Virgil. "I had opportunities offered to me that I never dreamed possible. I set up the fund especially for my people, but it's for anybody who wants it."

Miss Virgil was a bold pioneer who spent her life side-stepping the limitations of racism or combating in her own way its subtle or overtly hateful aspects. She was a woman of many talents and sang in several community and church choirs including North Congregational Church, York Congregational Church and the Rockingham Choral Group. Highly regarded for her leadership, Miss Virgil held a position on the UNH President's Council and volunteered at every opportunity, beginning in high school, with the Red Cross.

Collect Day 35 ❦ Elizabeth Ann Virgil

Oh loving God whose constant love surrounds us with your everlasting presence help us to be reminded of this in our daily lives: We follow in the steps of the Saints who have expressed their love for you with faith and action. Elizabeth Ann Virgil and her Mother Alberta Curry Virgil trusting in your faithful love encouraged learning and by their life example demonstrated to us who follow the certainty of Your love; Through Jesus Christ our Lord who lives and reins with you and the Holy Spirit, one God, now and forever. Amen.

Day 36
Keene, NH

Dr. Albert C. Johnson

(1900 – 1988)
Jeff Bolster

D R. ALBERT C. JOHNSON was born in 1900. An accomplished physician who practiced medicine for decades in Gorham and Keene, New Hampshire, Johnson had a welcoming smile. He never appeared to be mysterious. But Johnson had a secret.

Born and raised in Chicago, he matriculated at the University of Chicago's Rush Medical College – one of the most prestigious in the nation. While there he married a lovely young woman with a German name, Thyra Baumann. Upon graduating he secured an internship at the Maine General Hospital, in Portland. And when the General Practitioner in Gorham, New Hampshire died, opportunity knocked.

Gorham was a lovely town at the foot of the White Mountains. Dr. Johnson soon felt the special brand of craggy hospitality found in the North Country. A country doctor, he responded to summons at all hours. He set broken bones, pulled teeth and birthed babies. He joined Rotary and was elected to the School Board. The Johnsons and their children loved Gorham, but it was small. When the opportunity arose to study radiology at Harvard for a year, he took it. That led to a position in the hospital in Keene.

By then, war clouds were gathering. After Japan bombed Pearl Harbor, Americans lined up to serve. Dr. Johnson applied for a commission in the U.S. Navy. That would require a thorough background check. He gambled his secret would be safe.

A clean-cut young man from the Bureau of Naval Intelligence showed up. "We understand that even though you are registered as White, you have colored blood in your veins."

"Who knows what blood any of us has in our veins," replied the doctor.

The Navy knew. They denied Johnson a commission because of "inability to meet physical requirements." In other words, he wasn't 100% White.

Dr. Johnson and his wife had never intended to pass as White. Both were light-skinned, but both grew up knowing their Negro heritage. Johnson's father had been raised in Michigan, a very light-skinned man of color whose ancestors were free Blacks. His mother, also very light, knew both her parents had been Mississippi slaves. Thyra Baumann Johnson's German grandfather had emigrated to New Orleans, where he married a "colored" woman.

Both Johnsons had Negro friends and family members. Dr. Johnson had gone to medical school as a Negro. Rush Medical College had a quota — two Blacks per class. While there he joined a Black fraternity. Navy investigators easily uncovered that paper trail. He had only begun to live as White during his residency in Maine, because they would not have taken a Black doctor.

Throughout his life Johnson heard quizzical inquiries, triggered by his olive skin and wavy hair. "Do you think they are colored?" His son, Albert, Jr., got similar questions. At Mount Hermon, the exclusive prep school, his roommate put it bluntly "What are you?" "A kike or a Greek, or what? I bet you've got some nigger in you." But unlike his parents, who had been raised in the culture and society of light-skinned Blacks, Albert Jr. was just a White kid from Gorham, a good skier and member of the Congregationalist Church. Or so he thought.

The news affected every family member differently. Dr. Johnson's daughter, Anne, became anti-White. Dr. Johnson resigned from Rotary, and lost his zest for life, despite staying on at Keene Hospital. He was still respected but felt no longer fully accepted. "Whatever I do," he said, pointing to his credentials from the University of Chicago and Harvard, "my race gets no credit."

Albert Jr. slipped into depression. Would girls accept his advances? Would he have a career? A cross-country trip with a White kid who didn't care a bit that Albert was "colored" finally turned him around. They visited Albert's Black relatives in Los Angeles, and Albert dated a Black girl in Berkeley. Tensions abounded, but he came to accept himself, and ultimately enrolled at UNH.

Most White people in post-war America were ashamed of prejudices and tried not to show them, even as they felt that Blacks should know their place. Meanwhile, upper echelon Black society remained deeply suspicious of Whites. Dr. Johnson was not ashamed of being "colored," but to work, he had to pass. Ultimately, he and his family paid a steep price, right here in New Hampshire. Their choices, and their society's taboos, are worth pondering.

This true tale was the subject of a 1949 Hollywood film, *Lost Boundaries,* produced by Louis de Rochemont. Filming took place on location in Portsmouth, New Hampshire, Kittery and Kennebunkport, Maine, and Harlem, New York. The film was based on William Lindsay White's book of the same title.

Collect Day 36 ⚕ Dr. Albert C. Johnson

Almighty and everlasting God, by whose Spirit your faithful people are governed open our hearts to all people: Remind us to use the gifts that You have given us in the service of others without judgment. Show us through the lives of your saints that to give faithful service to your children is right and just. Teach us by the example of Dr. Johnson who gave freely of his medical skill and harnessed your healing power. Let us undo wherever we can any hint of racial prejudice and always practice your love; through Jesus Christ our Lord. Amen

Day 37
Manchester, NH

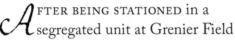

Lionel Johnson

(1923 – 2004)
Arnie Alpert

*A*FTER BEING STATIONED in a segregated unit at Grenier Field (now called Manchester-Boston Regional Airport) during World War II, Lionel Johnson decided Manchester would be a better place to raise a family than Louisiana, where he was born.

Manchester was not the Deep South, but neither was it entirely welcoming to African Americans in the 1950s and '60s. Housing and other forms of discrimination were common, so when discussion about starting a local branch of the NAACP started in 1964, Lionel was right there. Ten years later, he was right there again to bring the Greater Manchester Black Scholarship Foundation into being.

Lionel took over a dry-cleaning business, Fashion Cleaners, and ran it for more than forty years. He ran for and was elected to be a selectman, a local office involved in overseeing elections. He raised five daughters. And he established himself as a civic leader and as a go-to person for people concerned about civil rights violations. Though Lionel was never a "militant" in any sense of the word, it didn't take much agitation to stir things up in the Queen City, where politics were dominated by the publisher of *The Manchester Union Leader*, a supporter of segregation. Lionel's style was never about seeking confrontation, but over the years he acquired the skills, connections, and determination to help the small Black community stand up for dignified treatment by landlords, realtors, employers, educators and politicians.

When Coretta Scott King called for community observances to bolster the call for a national holiday on her late husband's birthday in 1983, Lionel was there again. As the NAACP branch president, he brought together leaders of the Scholarship Foundation and the Manchester YWCA to organize the city's first Martin Luther King Day event, held at Brookside Congregational Church during a raging blizzard. When Congress passed, and President Ronald Reagan signed legislation enacting a federal holiday named for Dr. King later that year, Lionel joined the rising call for New Hampshire to adopt a state holiday, too. Legislation to establish a King Holiday in New Hampshire had been first introduced — and defeated — in 1979. The same results occurred again in 1981, 1985, and 1987. By 1988, with frustration rising over New Hampshire's increasingly isolated status, Lionel united an informal association of Black civic leaders with labor and civil rights activists, educators and business leaders to mount the first organized push for the MLK state holiday. Known as the Martin Luther King Day Committee, Lionel became one of its chief leaders and spokespeople.

That year, Lionel also stepped down from his NAACP leadership role to seek and win office as a state representative, motivated largely by his desire to organize for the King holiday from the inside. The first robust effort to pass an MLK Day bill, in 1989 with Lionel as a co-sponsor, drew substantial support. But with active opposition from the editors of the Manchester newspaper, it failed again.

After being re-elected in 1990, Lionel tried again. This time, a bill to establish a New Hampshire holiday for Dr. King passed in the State Senate, but the House majority refused to go along. Along with the only other Black state representative that session, Lionel accepted a compromise bill to create a holiday known as "Civil Rights Day," an MLK Day alternative. Immediately, he and the MLK Day Committee began efforts to add Dr. King's name to the day. It took another eight years of steady campaigning, but with Rep. Lionel Johnson serving as a co-sponsor, a bill adding Dr. King's name to Civil Rights Day finally passed the NH House, 212 to 148, May 25, 1999. Lionel was proudly there on June 5 when Gov. Jeanne Shaheen signed it into law during a rally on the State House lawn.

Lionel Johnson was eighty-one years old when he died in his home on June 5, 2004. "It was about what he did," Lionel often said about Dr. King. In respect and appreciation for his commitment to educating young people about the African American freedom struggle, the Martin Luther King Coalition, which continues the tradition started in 1983 of holding annual MLK Day celebrations in Manchester, named the award for its Arts and Writing Contest after Lionel Johnson.

Collect Day 37 🎗 Lionel Johnson

Heavenly Father, in you we live and move and have our being: help us to remember at all times your earnest desire for justice for all your people; The gentle courage of your faithful servant Lionel Johnson laid the foundation for civil rights and equal opportunities regardless of birth. Leadership and thoughtful determination has allowed us who follow in his footsteps, signposts for the road ahead; through Jesus Christ our Lord. Amen.

Day 38
Portsmouth, NH

Lieut. Robert O. Goodman Jr.
(1956 –)
Valerie Cunningham

*O*N JAN. 2, 1984, LT. ROBERT O. GOODMAN JR., a twenty-seven-year-old Navy flier held by Syria for more than a month after having been shot down over Lebanon, arrived on an Air Force carrier in Washington where he was met by his wife and two young children.

The lieutenant was taken to the US Naval Medical Center to be examined. During a hectic morning that focused national attention on the Goodman family, Lt. Goodman's parents praised the Rev. Jesse Jackson on network news* for meeting with Syria's president and pressing for their son's release.

Mrs. Goodman said since her son was a young boy, he was interested in flying. His father was an Air Force lieutenant colonel stationed at a base in Puerto Rico where Robert was born. He was ten years old when the family transferred to New Hampshire. Mrs. Goodman said her son, who is five-feet eight-inches tall and slightly built, was a running back on the Portsmouth High School football team — "never a starter, but he always made the team." She said that although Goodman was not an outstanding student, he was determined and strong-willed.

He applied and graduated from the U.S. Naval Academy in 1978, became a navigator-bombardier and was assigned to Attack Squadron 85 when it sailed to Lebanon in October, 1983. Their mission was to drop 1,000-lb bombs on Syrian tanks and anti-aircraft in Lebanon, close to the Syrian border. On December 4th during an attack on Syrian positions east of Beirut, Lt. Goodman's two-seat A-6E Intruder was shot down by a surface-to-air missile. Both he and the pilot, Lt. Mark A. Lange, age twenty-six, of Fraser, Michigan, managed to eject and parachute out of the burning plane. The next thing Goodman remembered was being tied up and tossed in the back of a truck. He had no idea where he was being taken, or who his captors were. And it was only later that he learned that Lange died of his injuries.

"Once we got to Damascus, I was taken to a cell and then brought up for interrogation," he says. "I remember thinking very clearly — I have been cast into the middle of this conflict in the Middle East, which has been going on for hundreds, if not thousands, of years, and which I've been trying to solve with thousands of pounds of bombs." The Syrians were anxious to know about his bombing mission and Goodman was equally anxious not to tell them any details — or let on that he had been shot down before a single bomb had been dropped. "They weren't aggressive. They didn't threaten me. They were just persistent," he recalls. "It was stressful because I was trying to make stuff up, and also remember what I was making up in case they asked me about it again." Between interrogation sessions, he was left alone in his basement cell, with only a single light bulb and little sense of time. He feared that no-one outside knew what had happened to him.

In fact, news of his capture had spread quickly around the globe. The US government made numerous attempts to free him. From across America, people sent Christmas cards. He was visited by the US ambassador to Syria, and a delegation of religious leaders led by the Rev. Jesse Jackson, traveled to Damascus to petition President Hafez al-Assad for Goodman's release. Assad had decided to release Goodman, Jackson says, because it was in his interests to do so.

"It was a joyous moment," Lt. Goodman recalls, but what he felt most was "incredibly tired." He was feted as an American hero — a role, he did not feel comfortable with: "That's something I have never been able to reconcile. I didn't feel I had done something heroic. I look back on it as an interesting slice of time, but not something I conquered — rather as something I managed to get through." Goodman retired with the rank of commander in 1995.

*This story is adapted from reports in *The New York Times* and by the BBC.

Collect Day 38 ♈ Lieut. Robert O. Goodman Jr.

O God, creator and protector of all: We thank you for the courage of Lieut. Robert Goodman Jr. and the many soldiers of color who seek to protect this country while suffering at the hands of our perceived enemies. May his service and courage inspire others to work for peace and the safety of all humanity; through the blessing of Jesus Christ, your son, and our Lord. Amen.

Day 39
Portsmouth, NH

The Emerson Reed Family

Valerie Cunningham

*H*E WAS NOT the first nor the last high school graduate to miss a senior prom. There would be at least one of the Negro students attending Portsmouth High School in those days who would go to the prom. Usually it would be the Black girl, escorted either by her older brother or by the son of her mother's friend who lived in Newburyport or Portland. That's just the way it was. Not even Emerson Reed, a popular student and a track star, could cross the color line to dance with a White classmate. Emmy had convinced himself that going to the prom was not that important.

Education and honest work, on the other hand, always have been highly valued aspirations among African Americans. Emmy's grandfather, Samuel Reed, had come to New England out of southern slavery as a child in 1865, a time when most of New Hampshire's former slaves (and memories of them) had died. Samuel had access to public education and became Portsmouth's first Black mail carrier. His son, Ralph, Emerson Reed's father, trained to become a skilled worker at the naval shipyard. Meanwhile, Emmy's mother, Mary, worked at home as a seamstress and she re-caned chairs to supplement the family income. When Emmy finished high school, the family still had the two older brothers in college, so his option was to apply for the Civilian Conservation Corp (CCC), a federal public work relief program that let young men learn a skill and earn a monthly allowance. Upon acceptance into the program, Emmy was sent to a CCC camp in New Hampshire. However, when he arrive there, the director said he had not been informed of Emerson's race and that the New Hampshire camp was designated by federal law for Whites only. Emmy was told he had to go to the CCC location in Maine that was for colored only.

This was legalized segregation, like in the South! Emerson Reed had known the racial tensions of de facto segregation as a normal way of life while he was growing up in small-town New Hampshire, those undefined inconveniences could be managed with preparation and persistence — or strategic evasions.

Emmy discovered leadership skills while living in the Maine woods with young men whose normalcy had been shaped by the institutional racism that restricted urban ghettos. And he overcame culture shock after enlisting in the still-segregated military service only to find himself being dehumanized by crude and angry White men, then shunned by suspicious Black men who seemed to think he was from "another world". But Emmy made the best of his opportunities.

Whether succeeding in the CCC, helping to integrate the military, advancing to the first African American shop supervisor back home at the shipyard, or serving as a founding member on the shipyard's Equal Employment Opportunities board, Emmy would be ready. So, it was in 1958 when he served as president of New Hampshire's first branch of the NAACP and helped the community meet the housing crisis created by the opening of Pease Air Force Base. As the new racial "balance" challenged the status quo across the region, Emerson Reed, as NAACP Legal Redress Officer, became known as a voice of reason, ready to take legal action when needed. His skillful interactions with the public and the press helped set the tone for the peaceful integration of area barber shops, housing rentals and mobile home parks; and on July 4, 1964, as the U.S. Civil Rights Act went into effect, it was non-White Emmy and wife, Jane, who were seated with their non-Black UNH friends in the historic dining room of a landmark seaside hotel that, until that star-spangled moment, had not allowed African American guests or workers on the premises.

The Reed family tradition of pro-active community service continued when a daughter succeeded Emmy as president of the local NAACP. Sheila is now a member of the national organization called Coming to the Table — oh, and the DAR.

Collect Day 39 ❦ The Emerson Reed Family

O blessed God, whose desire is that all humans be seen as equal in each other's eyes: help us to remember the dedication and courage of Emerson Reed and his family as they worked to navigate racial tensions in order to be of service and integrate organizations and the military in New Hampshire and beyond. May we continue to honor their successes and struggles; through Jesus Christ who taught us to live together with love. Amen.

Day 40
Portsmouth, NH

Valerie Cunningham

Angela Matthews

A S A TEENAGER growing up in Portsmouth, Valerie Cunningham was proud of her family's African American heritage, but she was also curious about local Black history. While working at Portsmouth Public Library, she discovered Brewster's Rambles About Portsmouth. From Brewster's stories about local Blacks, Valerie found clues to a history that until then had been invisible. She began a quest that would consume the rest of her life as researcher, historian and chronicler of Black Portsmouth from 1645 to present day.

Valerie spent years documenting the stories of Africans and Black Americans through probate and church records, from broadsides and news archives at the Portsmouth Athenaeum and from oral histories she conducted with several Portsmouth Black elders.

More than any other individual, Valerie brought momentous change to Portsmouth and New Hampshire. Her work has influenced how the earliest African Americans are perceived, as courageous, determined, philanthropic and — most important — arriving on the block in 1645. She is described by local historian J. Dennis Robinson as the person who changed everything, referring to her book *Black Portsmouth* as "the bible."

In addition to her achievements as a public historian and preservationist, Valerie was also a founding member of the Seacoast

Council on Race and Religion (SCORR) convened by St. John's Episcopal Church and a diversity of community activists in response to the March 7, 1965 assault on civil rights demonstrators walking across the Edmund Pettus Bridge in Selma, Alabama, on what became known as Bloody Sunday. Meanwhile, Valerie also served a term as branch secretary of the Seacoast National Association for the Advancement of Colored People (NAACP) which her parents had helped to start in 1959.

Cunningham's first publication describing slavery in the colonial seaport appeared in the quarterly journal, *Historic New Hampshire*, in 1989. During the 1990s, Valerie's work was expanded as a curriculum guide with co-author, Mark J. Sammons, and distributed to the region's schools and libraries; then, again with Sammons, the book *Black Portsmouth: Three Centuries of African American Heritage* was published in 2004. In addition, Valerie led efforts to establish the Portsmouth Black Heritage Trail with the installation of two dozen bronze historic site markers all around Portsmouth. Her purpose in documenting and making visible this forgotten past is to remind us all of what is possible.

Collect Day 40 ☫ Valerie Cunningham

O Almighty God, the strength of all who put their trust in you: grant that we may honor the work of Valerie Cunningham, who brought to light the history of the Black community in Portsmouth, NH. Through her dedication to the truth may others be able to recognize the achievements and contributions that many people in the Black community have brought to the State of New Hampshire; through Christ our Lord, in the unity of the Holy Spirit, now and forever. Amen.

Thank you for reading!

You can help support these and other efforts like it—
Visit
BlackHeritageTrailNH.org
for a listing of our activities, including:
Elinor Williams Hooker Tea Talk Series
Statewide Sankofa Guided Walking, Trolley, and Bus Tours
Juneteenth Celebration
Black New England Conference
Lenten Program
Spring Symposium
Reading Frederick Douglass
School Collaborations and Preservation Projects
Historic and Cultural Preservation

Made in the
USA
Middletown, DE